Minstrel Henry

The Metrical History of Sir William Wallace, Knight of Ellerslie

Vol. II

Minstrel Henry

The Metrical History of Sir William Wallace, Knight of Ellerslie
Vol. II

ISBN/EAN: 9783744748643

Printed in Europe, USA, Canada, Australia, Japan

Cover: Foto ©ninafisch / pixelio.de

More available books at **www.hansebooks.com**

THE METRICAL HISTORY OF SIR WILLIAM WALLACE, KNIGHT OF ELLERSLIE,

BY HENRY, COMMONLY CALLED BLIND HARRY:

CAREFULLY TRANSCRIBED FROM THE M.S. COPY OF THAT WORK, IN THE *ADVOCATES' LIBRARY*, UNDER THE EYE OF THE EARL OF BUCHAN.

AND NOW PRINTED FOR THE FIRST TIME, ACCORDING TO THE ANCIENT AND TRUE ORTHOGRAPHY.

WITH NOTES AND DISSERTATIONS.

IN THREE VOLUMES.

VOL. II.

" A! Fredome is a nobill thing!
" Fredome maks a man to have lykinge,
" Fredome all folace to men gives,
" He lives at efe that freely lives!
  BARBOUR'S BRUS.

PERTH:
PRINTED BY R. MORISON JUNIOR,
FOR R. MORISON AND SON, BOOKSELLERS; PERTH.
M,DCC,XC.

THE LIFE

OF

Sir WILLIAM WALLACE, &c.

BOOK. VII.

Wallace fees a Vifion—Burns the Barns of Air—Puts Bifhop Beik out of Glafgow—Kills Lord Peircie—Goes to Lorn againſt Macfadzan—Kills Macfadzan—Takes Perth—At Aberdeen—Burns Dunotter—Drives Lord Beaumont out of Buchan—Befieges Dundee—Battle of Stirling—Sir Criftal Seton Kills Herbottle.

IN Feuerzher—befell ye famyn cace,
　Yat Inglifmen tuk trewis with Wallace.
Yis paffyt our till March till end was focht.
Ye Inglifmen keft all ye wayis yai mocht,
With futtelte, and wykkit illufione, 5
Ye worthi Scotts to put to confufioune;
In Aprill ye king of Ingland come
In Cummyrland off Pomfrat fro hys home;
Into Carleill till a confell he zeid,
Quharoff ye Scotts mycht haiff full mekill dreid; 10

Mony

Mony Captayne yat was off Ingland born,
Yidder yai paſt, and ſemblyt yar king beforn;
Na Scotts man till yat cunſaill yai cald,
Bot Schyr Amar, yat traytour was off ald.
At hym yai ſperd, how yai ſuld tak on hand,   15
Ye rychtwyſs blud to ſcour out off Scotland.
Schyr Amar ſaid, yair Chyftane can weill do,
Rycht wyſs in wer, and has gret power to;
And now yis trew giffs yaim ſic hardyment,
Yat to your faith yai will nocht all conſent :   20
Bot wald yow do rycht as I wald yow ler,
Yis peſs to yaim it ſuld be ſald full der.
Yan demyt he, ye fals Sothroune amang,
How yai mycht beſt ye Scotts Barownis hang.
For gret barnys yat tyme ſtud intill Ayr,   25
Wrocht for ye king, quhen hys lugyng was yar,
Byggyt about, yat no man entir mycht,
Bot ane at anys, nor haiff off oyir ſicht,
Yar ordand yai yir lords ſuld be ſlayne,
A juſtice maid, quhilk was of mekill mayne.   30
To Lord Perſye off yis mattir yai laid.
With ſad awyſs agayne to yaim he ſaid,
Yai men to me has kepyt treuth ſa lang,
Deſaitfully I may nocht ſe yaim hang.
I am yar fa, and warn yaim will I nocht,   35
Sa I be quytt, I rek nocht quhat be wrocht;
Fra ynce I will, and towart Glaſkow draw,
With our Bbſchope to her off hys new law.
Yan cheſyt yai a juſtice fers and fell,
Quhilk Arnulff hecht, as my auctour will tell,   40

Off

Off South-hamtoune, yat huge hie her and Lord,
He undirtuk to pyne yaim with ye cord.
Ane oyir in Glafkow ordand yai,
For Cliddifdaill men, to ftand yat famyn day;
Syne chargyt yaim, in all wayis erneftfully, 45
Be no kyne meyne Wallace fuld not chaip by:
For weill yai wyft, and yai men war owrthrawin,
Yai mycht at will bruk Scotland as yair awin.
Yis band yai cloifs undir yair feillis faft,
Syne fouth our mur agayn King Edward paft. 50
Ye new juftice refawit was in Ayr.
Ye Lord Perfye can on to Glafkow fayr.
Yis Ayr was fet in Jun ye auchtand day,
And playnly feryt, na fre man war away.
Ye Scotts marweld, and pefs tane in ye land, 55
Quhy Inglifmen fic maiftir tuk on hand.
Schyr Ranald fet a day befor yis Ayr,
At Monktoune kyrk, hys freynds mett hym yar.
William Wallace on to ye tryft couth pafs,
For as yan Wardane off Scotland he was. 60
Yis maiftir Jhon a worthi clerk was yar,
He chargyt hys kyne for to byd fra yat Ayr;
Rycht weill he wyft, fra Perfye fled yat land,
Gret perell was to Scotts apperand.
Wallace fra yaim to ye kyrk he zeid, 65
Pater Nofter, Aue, he faid, and Creid;
Syne to ye grete he lenyt hym fobyrly,
Apon a fleip he flaid full fodandly.
Kneland folowed, and faw hym fallyn on fleip,
He maid no noyis, bot wyfly couth hym kepe. 70

In yat flummir cummand hym thocht he faw,
Ane agyt man faft towart hym couth draw,
Sone be ye hand he hynt hym haiftele,
I am, he faid, in wiage chargyt with ze.
A fuerd hym gaiff off burly burnyft fteill,   75
Gud fone, he faid, yis brand zow fall bruik weill.
Off topaftone hym thocht ye plumat was,
Bathe hilt and hand all glitterand lik ye glas.
Der fon, he faid, we tary her to lang,
Yow fall go fe quhar wrocht is mekill wrang;   80
Yan he hym led till a montane on hycht,
Ye warld hym thocht he mycht fe with a fycht.
He left hym yar, fyne fone fra hym he went.
Yaroff Wallace ftudyt in hys entent,
Till fe hym mar he had ftill gret defyr,   85
Yarwith he faw begyne a felloune fyr,
Quhilk braithly brynt on breid throw all ye land,
Scotland atour, fra Rofs to Sulway fand.
Yan fone till hym yar defcendyt a queyne,
In lumyt, lycht, fchynand full brycht and fcheyne;   90
In hyr prefens apperyt fa mekill lycht,
Yat all ye fyr fche put out off hys fycht,
Gaiff hym a wand off colour reid and greyne,
With a faffyr fanyt hys face and eyne,
Welcum, fche faid, I cheifs ze as my luff,   95
Yow ar grantyt be ye gret God abuff,
Till help pepill yat fuffers mekill wrang,
With ye as now I may nocht tary lang,
Yow fall return to yi awne oyfs agayne,
Yi derraft kyn ar her in mekill payne;   100

Yis

Yis rycht regioune yow mon redeme it all,
Yi laſt reward in erd fall be bot ſmall;
Let nocht yarfor, tak redreſs off yis myſs,
To yi reward yow fall haiſt leſtand blyſs.
Off hyr rycht hand ſche betaucht hym a buk,   105
Humilly yus hyr leyff full ſone ſche tuk,
Into ye cloud aſcendyt off hys ſycht.
Wallace brak up ye buk in all hys mycht.
In thre parts ye buk weill wrytten was,
Ye fyrſt writtyng was groſs lettris of bras,   110
Ye ſecund gold, ye thrid was ſiluer ſcheyne.
Wallace merweld quhat yus writtyng ſuld meyne;
To rede ye buk he beſyet hym ſa faſt,
Hys ſpreit agayne to walkand mynd is paſt,
And up he raiſs, ſyne ſowndly furth went,   115
Yis clerk he fand, and tald hym hys entent
Off yis wiſioune, as I haiff ſaid befor,
Completly throuch, quhat neds words mor.
Der ſon, he ſaid, my witt unabill is
To ranſik ſic, fer dreid I ſay off miſs;   120
Zeit I ſall deyme, yocht my cummyng be ſmall,
God grant na charge eftir my words fall.
Sanct Androw was gaiff ze yat ſuerd in hand,
Off Sancts he is ye wowar off Scotland;
Yat montane is, quhar he ze had on hycht,   125
Knawlage to haiff off wrang yat yow mon rycht;
Ze fyr ſall be fell tithyngs, or ye part,
Quhilk will be tald in mony ſundry art.
I can nocht witt quhat queyne at it ſuld be,
Quheyr fortoun, or our lady ſo fre,   130

A 3   Lykly

Lykly it is, be ye brychtnes fche brocht,
Modyr off hym yat all yis warld has wrocht.
Ye pritty wand, I trew, be myne entent,
Affignes rewlle and cruell jugement;
Ye red colour, quha graithly underftud,   135
Betaknes all to gret battaill and blud;
Ye greyn, curage, yat yow art now amang,
In ftrowbill wer yow fall conteyne full lang;
Ye faphyr ftayne fche bliffit ye with all,
Is leftand Grace, will God, fall to yow fall;   140
Ye thrynfald buk is bot yis brokyn land,
Yow mon rademe be worthines off hand;
Ye bras lettris betakynnys bot to yis,
Ye gret opprefs off wer and mekill myfs,
Ye quhilk yow fall bryng to ye rycht agayne,   145
Bot yow yarfor mon fuffer mekill payne;
Ye gold takynnis honour and worthines,
Wictour in armys, yat yow fall haiff be grace;
Ye filuer fchawis cleyne lyff and hewynys blyfs,
To yi reward yat myrth yow fall nocht myfs,   150
Dreid nocht yarfor, be out off all dyfpayr.
Foryir as now heroff I can no mair.
He thankyt hym, and yus hys leyff has tayne,
Till Corfbe fyne with hys uncle raid hayme;
With myrthis yus all nycht yai foiornyt yar,   155
Apon ye morn yai graith yaim to ye Ar,
And furth yai ryd, quhill yai come to Kingace,
With dreidfull hart yus fperyt wycht Wallace
At Schyr Ranald, for ye chartir off pefs.
Neuo, he faid, yir words ar nocht les,   160

It

It is lewyt at Corſbe in ye kyſt
Quhar yow it laid, yaroff na othyr wiſt.
Wallace anſuerd, had we it her to ſchaw,
And yai be falſs, we ſuld nocht entir aw.
Der ſone, he ſaid, I pray zow paſs agayne, 165
Youch you wald ſend, yat trawaill war in wayne,
Bot yow or I, can nane it bryng yis tyde.
Gret Grace it was maid hym agayne to ryde.
Wallace raturnd, and tuk with hym bot thre,
Nane off yaim knew yis endentour but he. 170
Unhap hym led, forbid hym couth he nocht,
Off fals diſſayt yis gud knycht had na thocht.
Schyr Ranald raid, but reſtyng to ye toune,
Wittand na thing off all yis fals treſoune,
Yat wykked ſyng ſo rewled ye plainait, 175
Saturn was yan intill hys heaſt ſtait,
Aboun Juno in hys melancoly,
Jupiter Mars ay cruell off inwy;
Saturn as yan awanſyt hys natur,
Off terandry he power had and cur, 180
Rebell rewls in mony ſeir regioun,
Trubill weddyr makis ſchippis to droun;
Hys drychyn is with Pluto in ye ſe,
As off ye land, full off iniquite,
He waknys wer, waryng off peſtilence, 185
Fallyng off walls with cruell wiolence,
Puſoun is ryff, amang ye oyir things,
Sodeyn ſlauchter off emprours and kings;
Quhen Sampſone powed to grond ye gret piller,
Saturn was yan intill hys heaſt ſper; 190

At

At Thebes als off hys power yai tell,
Quhen Phiorax fank throch ye Erd till hell;
Off ye Troians he had full mekill cur,
Quhen Achilles at Troy flew gud Ectur;
Burdeous fchent, and mony citeis mo, 195
Hys power zeit it has na hap to ho;
In braid Brytane feill wengeance has beyne feyne,
Off yis and mar, ze wait weill quhat I meyne.
Bot to yis houfs, yat ftalwart was and ftrang,
Schyr Ranald come, and mycht nocht tary lang. 200
A bawk was knyt all full off rapys keyne,
Sic a towboth fen fyne was neuir feyne;
Stern men was fet ye entre for to hald,
Nayne mycht pafs in, bot ay as yai war tald.
Schyr Ranald fyrft to mak fewte for hys land, 205
Ye knycht went in, and wald na langar ftand;
A rynnand cord yai flewit our hys hed,
Hard to ye bawk, and hangyt hym to ded.
Schyr Bryfs ye Blair next with hys Eyme in paft,
On to ye ded yai haiftyt hym full faft, 210
Be he entryt hys hed was in ye fnar,
Tyit to ye bawk hangyt to ded rycht yar.
Ye thrid entrit, yat pete was for thy,
A worthi knycht, Schyr Neill Mungummry;
And oyir feill off landyt men about, 215
Mony zeid in, bot na Scotts come out
Off Wallace paft, yai put to yat derff deid;
Mony Crawfurd fa endyt in yat fteid.
Off Carrik men Kennadyfs flew yai als,
And kynd Cambells yat neuir had beyne falfs, 220

Y ir

Yir rabellit nocht contrar yir rychtwyſs croun,
Sothroune for yi yaim put to confuſioun.
Berklais, Boids, and Stuarts off gud kyn;
Na Scott chapyt yat tyme yat entrit in.
Upon ye bawk yai hangyt mony par, 225
Beſid yann ded in ye nuk keſt yaim yar.
Sen ye fyrſt tyme yat ony wer was wrocht,
To ſic a dede ſo mony ſic zeid nocht
Upon a day, throuch curſſit ſaxons ſeid;
Wengeance off yis throuchout yat Kynryk zeid. 230
Grantyt was fra God in ze gret Hewyn,
Sa ordand he yat law fuld be yair ſtewyn,
To falſs Saxons, for yair fell jugement,
Yar wykkydnes our all ye land is went.
Zhe nobill men, yat ar off Scotts kind, 235
Yar petous dede ze kepe into zour mynd,
And us rawenge, quhen we ar ſet in thrang.
Dolour it is heron to tary lang.
Yus auchteyn ſcor to yat derff dede yai dycht,
Off barronis bauld, and mony worthi knycht. 240
Quhen yai had ſlayne ye worthiaſt yat was yar,
For waik pepill yai wald na langar ſpar,
Intill a garth keſt yaim out off yat ſted,
As yai war born, dispulzeit, bar, and ded.
Gud Robert Boyd on till a tawern zeid, 245
With twenty men yat douchty war in deid,
Off Wallace houſs full cruell in entent,
He gouernyt yaim quhen Wallace was abſent.
Kerle turnyt with hys maiſtir agayne,
Kneland and Boyd, yat mekill war in mayne. 250

Stewyn

Stewyn off Irland went furth, upon ye ftreit
A trew woman full fone with hym couth meit.
He fparyt at hyr, quhat hapnyt in ye ayr.
Sorou, fche faid, is nothing ellis yar.
Ferdly fche aft, allace, quhar is Wallace? 255
Fra us agayne he paffyt at Kingace.
Go warn hys folk and haift yaim off ye toune,
To kepe hymfelf I fall be reddy boune.
With hyr as yan no mar tary he maid,
Till hys fallowis he went withoutyn baid, 260
And to yaim tald off all yis gret mysfair,
To Laglane wode yai bownyt withoutyn mar.
Be yis Wallace was cummand wondir faft,
For hys freynds he was full far agaft.;
On to ye bern fadly he couth perfew, 265
Till entir in, for he na perell knew.
Yis woman yan upon hym loud can call,
O fers Wallace, feill tempeft is befall,
Our men ar flayne, yat pete is to fe,
As beftiall hunds hangyt our a tre, 270
Our trew barrouns be twa and twa paft in.
Wallace wepyt for gret lofs off hys kyn,
Yan with unefs apon hys horfs he baid,
Mair for to fper to yis woman he raid.
Der nece, he faid, ye trewth giff yow can tell, 275
Is my Eyme dede, or how ye cace befell.
Out off zon bern, fche faid, I faw hym born,
Nakit, laid law on cald erd me beforn;
Hys frofty mouth I kiffit in yat fted,
Rycht now manlik, now bar, and brocht to ded, 280

And

And with a claith I coweryt hys licaym,
For in hys lyff he did neuir woman fchayme.
Hys fyftirs fone you art, worthi and wycht,
Rawenge yar dede, for Godds faik, at yi mycht;
Als I fall help, as I am woman trew.   285
Der wycht, he faid, der, God fen at you knew
Gud Robert Boid, quhar at you can hym fe,
Wilzham Crawfurd als giff ye lyffand be,
Adam Wallace wald help me in yis ftriff,
I pray to God fend me all in liff;   290
For Marys faik bid yaim fone cum to me,
Ye juftice Innys yow fpy for cheryte,
And in quhat feir yat yai yair lugyng mak,
Sone eftir yat we will our purpofs tak
Into Laglane, quhilk has my fuccour beyne,   295
Adew Market, and welcum wodds greyne.
Heroff as yan till hyr he fpak no mair,
Hys brydill turnyt, and fra hyr can he fair;
Sic murnyng maid for hys der worthi kyn,
Hym thocht for baill yis breyft ner bryft in twyn. 300
As he yus raid in gret angyr and teyne,
Off Inglifmen yar folowed hym fyfteyn,
Wycht, waillyt men, yat towart hym couth draw,
With a mafer, to tack hym to ye law.
Wallace raturnd, in greiff and matelent,   305
With hys fuerd drawyn amang yaim fone he went.
Ye myddyll off ane he mankit ner in twa,
Ane oyir yar apon ye hed can ta,
Ye thrid he ftraik, and throuch ye coft hym claiff,
Ye ferd to ground rycht derfly ded doune he draiff,

Ye

Ye fyfft he hit with gret ire in yat fted,
Without refkew dreidles he left yaim ded,
Yan hys thre men had flayn ye toyir fyffe;
Fra yaim ye laiff efchapyt into lyff,
Fled to yair Lord, and tald hym off yis cace. 315
To Laglane wode yan rids wycht Wallace.
Ye Sothroune faid, quhat ane yat he hyt rycht,
Without merce, dredles to ded was dycht.
Merwell yai had fic ftrenth in ane fuld be,
Ane off yair men at ilk ftraik he gert de. 320
Yin demyt yai it fuld be Wallace wycht.
To yar langage maid anfuer ane ald knycht,
Forfuth, he faid, be he chapyt yis Ayr,
All your new deid is eking off our cayr.
Ye juftice faid, quhen yar fic murmur raifs, 325
Ze wald be ferd, and yar come mony faifs,
Yat for a man methink you lik to fle,
And wait nocht zett in deid gyff it be he;
And yocht it be, I count hym bot full lyeht,
Quha bids her ilk gentillman fall be knycht: 330
I think to deill yair lands haill to morn
To yow about, yat ar off Ingland born.
Ye Sothroune drew to yair lugyng bot mar,
Four thoufand haill yat nycht was intill Ayr.
In gret bernyfs, biggyt without ye toune, 335
Ye juftice lay, with mony bald baroune;
Yan he gert cry about yai waynys wyde,
Na Scotts born amang yaim yar fuld byde.
To ye caftell he wald nocht pafs for eyfs,
Bot foiornd yar with thing yat mycht hym pleyfs. 340

Great

Great purweans be fe to yaim was brocht,
With Irland ayle ye mychtcaft couth be wrocht.
Na wach was fet, becaufs yai had na dout
Off Scotts men yat leiffand was without;
Lawberand in mynd yai had beyn all yat day, 345
Off ayle and wyne yneuch chofyne haiff yai:
As beftly folk tuk off yaimfclff no keip,
In yair brawnys fone flaid ye fleuthfull fleip,
Throch full gluttre in fwarff fwappyt lik fwyn,
Yair Chyftane yan was gret Bachus off wyn. 350
Yis wyfs woman befy amang yaim was,
Feill men fche warnd and gert to Laglane pafs,
Hyrfclff formeft, quhill yai with Wallace met,
Sum comfort yan intill hys mynd was fet;
Quhen he yaim faw he thankyt God off mycht, 355
Tithands he aft, ye woman tald hym rycht,
Slepand as fwyn ar all yon fals menzhe,
Na Scotts man is in yat cumpane.
Yan Wallace faid giff yai all drokyn be,
I call it beft with fyr for yaim to fe. 360
Off gud men yan thre hundreth till hym focht;
Ye woman had tald thre trew burges at brocht,
Out off ye toune, with nobill ayle, and breid,
And oyir ftuff, as mekill as yai mycht leid.
Ye eit and drank ye Scotts men yat mocht. 365
Ye nobils yan Jop has to Wallace brocht,
Sadly he faid, der freynds now ze fe
Our kyne is flayne, yaroff is gret pete,
Throuch feill murthyr, ye gret difpite is mor,
Now fum rameid I wald we fet yarfor. 370

Suppofs yat I was maid Wardane to be,
Part ar away fic chargs put to me,
And ze ar her cummyn off als gud blud,
Als rychtwyfs born, be awentur and als as gud,
Als forthwart, fair, and als likly off perfoun, 375
As euir was I; yarfor till conclufioun,
Latt us cheyfs fyfc off yis gud cumpane,
Syne caflis caft quha fall our maifter be.
Wallace and Boyd, and Crawfurd off renoun,
And Adam als yan Lord off Ricardtoune, 380
Hys fadyr yan was wefyed with fekncs,
God had hym tayne intill his leftand Grace;
Ye fyft Awchinlek in wer a nobill man,
Caflis to caft about yir fyffe began.
It wald on hym, for ocht yai cuth dewyfs, 385
Continualy, quhill yai had caftyn thryfs.
Yan Wallace raifs, and out a fuerd can draw,
Ile faid, I wow to ye Makar off aw,
And till Mary, hys modyr wyrgyne cler,
My unclis dede now fall be fauld full der, 390
With mony man off our der worthi kyn,
Fyrft, or I eit or drynk we fall begyn,
For fleuth nor fleip fall nayn remayn in me,
Off yis tempeft till I awengeance fe.
Yan all inclynd rycht humyll off accord, 395
And hym refawit as Chyftane and yair Lord.
Wallace a lord he may be clepyt weill,
Yocht ruryk folk yaroff haiff litill feill,
Na deyme na lord, bot lands be yair part.
Had he ye warld, and be wrachit off hart, 400

He

He is no lord as to ye worthines,
It can nocht be, but fredome lord lyknes.
At ye rodds yai mak full mony ane,
Quhilk worthi ar, yocht lands haiff yai nane.
Yis difcuffyng I leiff herrolds till end, 405
On my mater now breiffly will I wend.
Wallace cummand a burgefs for to get,
Fyne cawk eneuch, yat hys der nece mycht fet
On ilk zeit, quhar Sothroune war on raw.
Yan twenty men he gert faft wetheis thraw, 410
Ilk man a pair, and on yair arme yaim threw,
Yan to ye toune full faft yai couth perfew.
Ye woman paft befor yaim futtelly,
Cawkit ilk zeit, yat yai neid nocht gang by.
Yan feftnyt yai with wetheis durs faft, 415
To ftapill and hefp, with mony fekyr caft.
Wallace gart Boyd ner hand ye caftell ga,
With fyfte men, a jeperte to ma.
Gyff ony ifchit ye fyr quhen yat yai faw,
Faft to zett he ordand yaim to draw. 420
Ye laiff with hym about ye bernys zheid.
Yis trew woman yaim feruit weill in deid,
With lynt and fyr, yai haiflely kendill wald,
In euir ilk nuk yai feftnyt blefs bald.
Wallace commaund till all hys men about, 425
Na Sothroune man at yai fuld lat brek out,
Quhat euir he be refkewis off yat kyn,
Fra ye rede fyr, hymfelff fall pafs yarin.
Ye lemand low fone lauffyt apon hycht.
Furfuth, he faid, yis is a pleffand fycht, 430

Till our harts it fuld be fum radrefs,
War yir away, yar power war ye lefs.
On to ye juftice hymfelff fone loud can caw,
Lat us to borch our men fra zour fals law,
At leyffand ar, yat chapyt fra zour ayr, 435
Deyll nocht yar land, ye unlaw is our fayr,
Yow bad no rycht, yat fall be on ze feyne.
Rewmour raifs with cairfull cry and keyne.
Ye bryme fyr brynt rycht braithly apon loft,
Till flepand men yat walkand was nocht foft. 440
Ye fycht without was awfull for to fe:
In all ye warld na grettar payne mycht be,
Yan yai within fufferyt for to duell,
Yat euir was wrocht, bot purgatory or hell.
A payne off hell weill ner it mycht be cauld, 445
Mad folk with fyr hampryt in mony hauld.
Feill byggyns brynt, yat worthi war and wycht,
Gat nane away, knaiff, captane, nor knycht.
Quhen brands fell off rafftreis yaim amang,
Sum rudly raifs in byttir paynys and ftrang, 450
Sum nakyt brynt, but beltlefs all away,
Sum neuir raifs, bot fmoryt quhar yai lay;
Sum rufchyt faft till Ayr giff yai mycht wyn,
Blyndyt in fyr, yair deidis war full off dyn.
Ye reik mellyt with fylth off carioune, 455
Amang ye fyr, rycht foull off offenfioune,
Ye pepill beryt lik wyld beftis in yat tyde,
Within ye wallis rampand on ayir fyd,
Rewmyd in reuth, with mony gryfly greyne,
Sum grymly gret, quhill yair lyff dayis war gayne;

Sum

Sum durs focht ye entre for to get,
Bot Scotts men so wyfly yaim befet,
Gyff ony brak, be awentur, off yat ftede,
With fuerds fone bertnyt yai war to dede,
Or ellis agayn be forze drewyn in ye fyr; 465
Yar chapyt nayne bot brynt up bayne and lyr.
Ye ftynk fcalyt off dede bodyis fa wyde,
Ye Scotts abhord ner hand for to byd,
Zeid to ye wynd, and leit yaim ewyn allayne,
Quhill ye rede fyr had yat fals blud ourgayne. 470
A Frer, Drumlay, was Priour yan off ayr,
Sewyn fcor with hym yat nycht tuk herbry yar,
In his innys, for he mycht not yaim let,
Till ner mydnycht a wach on yaim he fet,
Sum mendis he thocht to tak off yat fuppryfs, 475
Hymfelff wouk weill quhill he ye fyr fa ryfs.
Hys broyrs fewyn till harnes fone yai zeid,
Hymfelff Cheftayne ye remanand to leid.
Ye beft yai waill off armour and gud ger,
Syne wapynnys tak, rycht awfull in affer. 480
Yir aucht frers in four parts yai ga,
With fuerds drawyn, till ilk houfs zeid twa.
Sone entryt yai quhar Sothroune flepand war,
Apon yaim fett with ftraikis fad and far;
Feill frekis yar yai frers dang to dede, 485
Sum nakit fled, and gat out off yat fted,
Ye wattir focht, abaiffit out off flepe,
In ye furd weill, yat was bath wan and depe,
Feill off yaim fell, yat brak out off yat place,
Dowkit to grounde, and deit withoutyn grace. 490

B 3   Drownyt

Drownyt and flayne war all yat harbryt yar,
Men callis it zeit, ye freris blyffyng off Ayr.
Few folk off waill was lewyt upon cace
In ye Caftell; Lord Perfye fra yat place,
Befor ye Ayr, fra ynce to Glafkow drew,   495
Off men and ftuff it was to purwa new;
Zeit yai within faw ye fyr byrnand ftout,
With fchort awyfs ifchit, and had na doubt.
Ye bufchement yan, as weryouris wifs and wycht,
Leit yaim allayne, and to ye houfs paft rycht;   500
Boid wan ye port, entryit and all hys men,
Keparis in it was left bot nyne or ten;
Ye formaft fone hymfelff fefyt in hand,
Maid guyt off hym, fyne flew all yat yai fand.
Off purweance in yat Caftell was nayne,   505
Schort tyme befor Perfye was fra it gayne.
Ye Erle Arnulff had refawit yat hauld,
Quhilk in ye toun was brynt to powder cauld.
Boyd gert ramayn off hys men twenty ftill,
Hymfelff paft furth to witt off Wallace will,   510
Kepand ye toun, quhill nocht was lewyt mar,
Bot ye wode fyr, and beylds brynt full bar.
Off lykly men, yat born was in Ingland,
Be fuerd and fyr yat nycht deit fyffe thoufand.
Quhen Wallace men was weill togyddir met,   515
Gud freinds, he faid, ye knaw yat yar was fet
Sic law as yis now into Glafkow toune,
Be Byfchope Beik, and Perfye off renoune,
Yarfor I will in haift we yidder fair,
Off our gud kyn part ar loffyt yar.   520

He gert full fone ye burges till hym call,
And gaiff cummand in general to yaim all,
In kepyng yai fuld tak ye houfs off Ayr,
And hald it haill quhill tyme yat we her mayr;
To byd our king caftellys I wald we had, 525
Caft we doune all, we mycht be demyt ourrad.
Yai gart meit cum, for yai had faftyt lang,
Litill he tuk fyne bownyt yaim to gang.
Horfs yai cheyfs, yat Sothroune had brocht yar,
Anew at will, and off ye toune can fair; 530
Thre hundreth haill was in hys cumpany,
Rycht wondir faft raid yis gud chewalry
To Glafkow bryg, yat byggyt was off tre,
Weill paffit owr or Sothroune couth yaim fe.
Lord Perfye wyft, yat befy was in wer, 535
Semblyt hys men fell awfull in effer;
Yan demyt yai yat it was wycht Wallace,
He had befor chapyt throw mony cace.
Ye Byfchope Beik and Perfye yat was wycht,
A thoufand led off men in armyfs brycht. 540
Wallace faw weill quhat nowmyr femblyt yar,
He maid hys men in twa parts to fair,
Graithit yaim weill without ye tounys end.
He callyt Awchinlek for he ye paffage kend,
Uncle, he faid, be befy into wer, 545
Quheyr will ze ye Byfchopis taill upber,
Or pafs befor, and tak hys benyfone.
He anfuerd hym, with rycht fchort prowifione,
Unbyfchoppyt zeit, for futh I trow you be,
Yourfelff fall fyrft hys blyffing tak for me, 550
For

For fekyrly ze feruit it beft ye nycht;
To ber hys taill we fall in all our mycht.
Wallace anfuerd fen we mon fyndry gang,
Perell yar is and ze bid fra us lang,
For zone ar men will nocht fone be agaft,   555
Fra tyme we meit for God faik haift yow faft,
Our diffcueryng I wald na Sothroune faw,
Behynd yaim cum, and in the Northaft raw,
Gud men off wer ar all Northummyrland;
Yai partand yus tuk oyir be ye hand.   560
Awchinlek faid, we fall do at we may,
We wald lik ill to byd oucht lang away;
A bouftous ftaill betwix us fone mon be,
Bot to ye rycht all mycht God haiff e.
Adam Wallace and Awchinlek war boune,   565
Sewyn fcor with yaim on ye bak fyd ye toune;
Rycht faft yai zeid, quhill yai war out off fycht.
Ye toyir part arayit yaim full rycht,
Wallace and Boyd ye playne ftreit up can ga.
Sothroune marweld becaufs yai faw na ma,   570
Yar fenzhe cryit upon ye Perfyes fyde,
With Byfchope Beik yat bauldly durft abyde.
A fayr fembly was at yat metyng feyne,
As fyr on flynt it feyrryt yaim betweyne.
Ye hardy Scotts rycht awfully yaim abaid,   575
Brocht feill to ground throch weid yat weill was maid,
Perffyt platts with poynts ftiff off fteill,
Befor off hand gert mony cruell kneill.
Ye ftrang ftour raifs, as reik, upon yaim faft,
Or myft, throch fone, up to ye clouds paft.   580

To

To help yaimfelff ilk ane had mekill neid.
Ye worthi Scots ftud in felloune dreid,
Zet furthwart ay yai preffyt for to be,
And yai on yaim, gret wondyr was to fe.
Ye Perfeis men in wer was oyffit weill, 585
Rycht ferfly faucht and fonzeit nocht a deill.
Adam Wallace and Awchinlek com in,
And partyt Sothroune rycht fodeynly in twin,
Raturnd to yaim as nobill men in wer,
Ye Scotts gat rowme, and mony down ya ber; 590
Ye new countir affailziet yaim fa faft,
Throch Inglifmen maid floppys at ye laft.
Yan Wallace felff, into yat felloune thrang,
With hys gud fuerd, yat hewy was and lang,
At Perfyes face with a gud will he bar, 595
Bathe bayne and brayne ye forgyt fteill throch fchar.
Four hundreth men, quhen Lord Perfye was dede,
Out off ye gait ye Byfchope Beik yai lede,
For yan yaim thocht it was no tyme to byd,
By ye frers kirk, till a wode faft befyd. 600
In yat foreft forfuth yai taryt nocht,
On frefche horfs to Bothwell fone yai focht.
Wallace folowed with worthi men and wycht,
Forfouchtyn yai war and trewald all ye nycht,
Zeit feill yai flew into ye chace yat day, 605
Ye Byfchope felff and gud men gat away;
Amar Wallange refkewit hym in yat place,
Yat knycht full oft did gret harme to Wallace.
Wallace began off nycht ten hours in Ayr,
On day be nyne in Glafkow femblyt yair, 610

Be

Be ane our nowne at Bothwell zet he was,
Repreiffit Wallang or he wald foryir pafs;
Syne turnd agayne, as weyll witnes ye buk;
Till Dnudaff raid, and yar reftyng he tuk,
Tald gud Schyr Jhon off yair tythands in Ayr, 615
Gret mayne he maid he was nocht with hym yar.
Wallace foiornd in Dundaff at hys will,
Fyffe dayis owt, quhill tithands come hym till,
Out off ye hycht, quhar gud men was forlorn,
For Bowchane raifs, Adell, Menteth, and Lorn, 620
Apon Argyll a felloune wer yai mak,
For Edwards faik yus can yai undirtak.
Ye Knycht Cambell in Argyll yan was ftill,
With hys gud men agayn King Edwards will,
And kepyt fre Lowchow hys heretage, 625
Bot Makfadzan yan did hym gret owtrage.
Yis Makfadzan till Inglifmen was fuorn,
Edward gaiff hym bath Argyll and Lorn.
Falfs Jhon off Lorn to yat gyft can concord,
In Ingland yan he was new maid lord. 630
Yus falsfly he gaiff owr hys heretage,
And tuk at London off Edwarde grettar wage.
Duncan off Lorn zeitt for ye lands ftraiff,
Quhill Makfadzan ourfett hym with ye laiff,
Put hym off force to gud Cambell ye Knycht, 635
Quhilk into wer was worthi, wyfs and wycht.
Yus Makfadzan was entryt into Scotland,
And maruelufly yat tyrand tuk on hand,
With hys power, ye quilk I fpake off ayr,
Yai four lordfchippis all femblyt till hym yar; 640

Fyfteyne

Fyfteyne thousand off cursyt folk in deid,
Off all gaddryn, in oft he had to leid;
And mony off yaim was out off Irland brocht,
Barnys nor wyff yai pepill sparyt nocht,
Waistyt ye land als fer as yai mycht ga,   645
Yai beftly folk couth nocht bot byrn and fla.
Into Lowchow he entryt sodeynly,
Ye Knycht Cambell maid gud defens for yi;
Till Crage Vyum with thre hundir he zeid,
Yat ftrenth he held for all hys cruell deid,   650
Syne brak ye bryg, quhar yai mycht not out pafs,
Bot throuch a furd, quhar narow paſſage was;
Abandounly Cambell agayne yaim baid,
Faft apon Avifs yat was bathe depe and braid.
Makfadzan was apon ye toyir fyd,   655
And yar on force behuffyt hym for to byd;
For at ye furde he durft nocht entir out,
For gud Cambell mycht fet hym yan in dout.
Makfadzane focht, and a fmall paſſage fand,
Had he lafar, yai mycht pafs off yat land,   660
Betwix a roch and ye gret wattir fyd,
Bot four in frount na ma mycht gang nor ryd.
In till Lowchow was beftis gret plente,
A quhill he thocht yar with hys oft to be.
And oyir ftuff yat yai had with yaim brocht,   665
Bot all hys crafft awailzeit hym rycht nocht.
Dunkan off Lorn hás feyne ye fodeyne cace,
Fra gud Cambell he went to feik Wallace,
Sum helpe to get off yar turment and teyne;
Togydder befor in Dunde yai had beyne,   670
                         Lerand

Lerand at fcule into yair tendyr age,
He thockt to flaik Makfadzans curage.
Gylmychell yan with Dunkan furth hym dycht,
Agyd he was, and fute man wondyr wycht.
Sone can yai witt quhar Wallace lugyt was, 675
With yair cumplaynt to hys prefence yai pafs.
Erle Malcom als ye Lenox held at efs,
With hys gud men to Wallace can he prefs.
Till hym yar come gud Richard off Lundy.
Intill Dundaff he wald na langar ly, 680
Schyr Jhon ye Grayme als bownyt hym to ryde.
Makfadzans wer fa grewit yaim yat tyde,
At Wallace thocht hys gret power to fe,
In quhat aray he rewllit yat contre.
Ye Rukbe yan he kepyt with gret wrang, 685
Stirling Caftell yat ftalwart was and ftrang.
Quhen Wallace come be fowth it in a waill,
Till Erle Malcom he faid he wald affaill.
In diuerfs parts he gert feuer yar men,
Off yair power yat Sothroune fuld nocht ken. 690
Erle Malcom baid in bufchement out off fycht.
Wallace with hym tuk gud Schyr Jhon ye Knycht,
And a hundreth off wyfs wer men but doubt,
Throuch Stirlyng raid gyff ony wald yfche out;
Towart ye bryg ye gayneft way yai pafs. 695
Quhen Rukbs faw quhat at yair power was,
He tuk fewyn fcor of gud archars was yar,
Apon Wallace yai folowed wondyr far;
At fell bykkar yai did yaim mekill der.
Wallace in hand gryppyt a nobill fper, 700

Agayne

Agayne raturnd and has ye formaſt ſlayn.
Schyr Jhon ye Grayme, yat mekill was off mayne,
Amang yaim raid with a gud ſper in hand,
Ye fyrſt he ſlew yat he befor hym fand,
Apon anoyir hys ſper in ſondyr zeid, 705
A ſuerd he drew quhilk helpyt hym in neid.
Inglis archars apon yaim can ranew,
Yat hys gud horſs with arrowis ſone yai ſlew,
On fute he was. Qnhen Wallace has it ſeyne,
He lychtyt ſone, with men off armys keyne, 710
Amang ye rout fechtand full wondyr faſt.
Ye Ingliſmen raturnyt at ye laſt.
At ye Caſtell yai wald haiff beyne full fayne;
Bot Erle Malcom, with men off mekill mayne,
Betwix ye Sothroune and ye zeitts zeid, 715
Mony yai ſlew yat douchty was in deid.
In ye gret preſs Wallace and Rukbe met,
With hys gud ſuerd a ſtraik upon hym ſet,
Derfly to dede ye ald Rukbe he draiff,
Hys twa ſonnys chapyt amang ye laiff; 720
In ye Caſtell be awentur yai zeid,
With twenty men, na ma chapyt yat dreid.
Ye Lenox men, with yair gud Lord at was,
Fra ye Caſtell yai ſaid yai wald nocht paſs,
For weill yai wyſt it mycht nocht haldyn be. 725
On na lang tyme for yi yas ordand he.
Erle Malcom tuk ye houſs and kepyt yat tyd.
Wallace wald nocht fra hys fyrſt purpoſs byd,
Inſtance he maid to yis gud Lord and wyſs,
Fra ynce to paſs he ſuld in na kyn wyſs, 730

VOL. II.   C   Quhill

Quhill he had tane Stirlyng ye Caſtell ſtrang,
Trew men hym tald he mycht not hald it lang.
Yan Wallace thocht was maiſt on Makfadzane,
Off Scotts men he had ſlayne mony ane.
Wallace awowid, yat he ſuld wrokyn be, 735
On yat rebald, or ellis yarfor to de.
Off tyrandry King Edwarde thocht hym gud,
Law born he was, and off law ſimpill blud.
Yus Wallace was far grewyt in hys entent,
To yis jornay rycht ernyſtfully be went. 740
At Stirling Bryg aſſemblyt till hym rycht
Twa thouſand men yat worthi war and wycht.
Towart Argyll he bownyt hym to ryd,
Dunkan off Lorn was yair trew ſekyr gyd.
Off ald Rukbe, ye quhilk we ſpak off ayr, 745
Twa ſonnys in lyff in Stirling lewit yar;
Quhen yai broyirs conſawit weill ye rycht,
Yis houſs to hald yat yai na langar mycht,
For Cauſs quhi, yai wantyt men and meit,
With Erle Malcom yai keſt yaim for to treit, 750
Grace off yair lyff, and yai yat with yaim was;
Gaiff our ye houſs, ſyne couth in Ingland paſs,
On ye thrid day yat Wallace fra yaim raid.
With King Edwarde full mony zer yai baid,
In Brucs wer agayne come into Scotland, 755
Sterlyng to kepe ye tane off yaim tuk on hand.
Mentione off Bruce is oft in Wallace buk,
To fend hys rycht full mekill payne he tuk.
Quhar to ſuld I heroff tary ma,
To Wallace furth now ſchortlye will I ga. 760

Dunkan

Dunkan off Lorne, Gylmychall fra yaim fend,
A fpy to be, for he ye-contre kend,
Be our party was paffit ftraithfulan,
Ye fmall fute folk began to irk ilk ane,
And horfs, off fors, behuffyt for to faill; 765
Yan Wallace thoucht yat cumpany to waill,
Gud men, he faid, yat is nocht meit for us;
In brokyn ray, and we cum on yaim yus,
We may tak fcaith, and harmye our fayis bot fmall,
To yaim in lik we may nocht femble all; 770
Tary we lang a playne feild yai will get,
Apon yaim fone fa weill we may nocht fet;
Part we mon leiff as folowand for to be,
With me fall pafs our power into thre.
A hundyr fyrft till hymfelf he has tayne, 775
Off weftland men, was worthi knawin ilk ane.
To Schyr Jhon Grayme als mony ordand he,
And fyfe hundreth to Rychard off Lundy,
In yat part was Wallace off Ricardtoune,
In all gud deid he was ay reddy boune. 780
Fyfe hundreth left, yat mycht nocht with yaim ga,
Suppofs at yai to byd was wondyr wa.
Yus Wallace oft began to tak ye hycht,
Our a montayne fone paffit off yar fycht.
In Glendowchar yair fpy met yaim agayne, 785
With Lord Cambell, yan was our folk rycht fayne;
At yat metyng gret blythnes mycht be feyne,
Thre hundreth he led, yat cruell war and keyne.
He comford yaim, and bad yaim haiff na dreid,
Zon beftly folk wants wapynnys and weid, 790

Sone yai will fle, fcharply and we perfew.
Be Louthdouchyr full fodynlye yaim drew,
Yan Wallace faid, a lyff all fall we ta,
For her nane will fra hys falow ga.
Ye fpy he fend, ye entre for to fe, 795
Apon ye mofs a fcurrour fone fand he;
To fcour ye land Makfadzane had hym fend,
Out off Cragmor yat day he thocht to wend.
Gylmychall faft apon hym folowit yar,
With a gud fuerd, yat weill and fcharply fchar, 800
Maid quyt off hym, at tithands tald he nane,
Ye outfpy yus was loft fra Makfadzane.
Yan Wallace oft apon yair fute yai lycht,
Yair horfs yai left yocht yai war neuir fo wycht,
For mofs and crag yai mycht na langar dre; 805
Yan Wallace faid, quha gangs beft let fe.
Throuch out ye mofs delyuerly yai zeid,
Syne tuk ye hald quharoff yai had maift dreid;
Endlang ye fchoir ay four in frownt yai paft,
Quhill yai within affemblyt at ye laft. 810
Lord Cambell faid, we haiff chewyfs yis hauld,
I trow to God yair waukynyng fall be cauld;
Her is na gait to fle zone pepil can,
Bot rockis heich, and wattir depe and wan.
Auchtcyne hundreth off douchty men in deid, 815
On ye gret oft but mar procefs yai zeid,
Fechtand in frount, and mekill maiftry maid,
On ye frayit folk bufkyt withowtyn baid,
Rudly to ray yai rufchit yaim agayne,
Gret part off yaim was men off mekill mayne. 820
Gud

Gud Wallace men fa ftoutly can yaim fter,
Ye battaill on bak Fyfe akyr breid yai ber;
Into ye ftour feill tyrands gert yai kneill.
Wallace in hand had a gud ftaff off fteill,
Quhomeuir he hytt to ground brymly yaim bar, 825
Roind hym about a large rude and mar.
Schyr Jhon ye Grayme in deid was rycht worthy,
Gud Cambell als, and Rychard off Lundy,
Adam Wallace, and Robert Boid in feir,
Amang yair fayis, quhar deids was fald full der. 830
Ye felloune ftour was awfull for to fe;
Makfadzan yan fa gret debait maid he,
With Yrage men hardy and curageous,
Ye ftalwart ftryff rycht hard and paralous.
Boundance off blud fra woundis wyd and wan, 835
Stekyt to deid on ground lay mony man.
Ye ferfaft yar yneuch off fechtand fand,
Twa hours large into ye ftour yai ftand,
At Jop hymfelff weill wyft nocht quha fuld wyn:
Bot Wallace men wald nocht in fowndyr twyn, 840
Till help yaimfelff yai war off hardy will,
Off Yrage blud full hardely yai fpill,
With feill fechtand maid floppys throuch ye thrang.
On ye fals part our wycht wer men fa dang,
Yat yai to byd mycht haiff na langar mycht, 845
Ye Irland folk yan maid yaim for ye flycht,
On craggs clam and fum in wattir flett,
Twa thoufand yar drownyt withoutyn lett:
Born Scottfmen baid ftill into ye feild,
Keft wappynys fra yaim, and on yar kneis kneild, 850

C 3   With.

With petous woice yai cryit apon Wallace,
For Godds faik to tak yaim in hys Grace.
Grewit he was, bot rewth off yaim he had,
Refawyt yaim fayr with contenance full fad,
Off our awne blud we fuld haiff gret pete, 855
Luk ze fla nane off Scotts will zoldyn be,
Off outland men lat nane chaip with ye lyff.
Makfadzane fled, for all hys felloune ftryff,
On till a cave, within a clifft off ftayne,
Undyr Cragmor, with fyfteyne is he gayne. 860
Dunkan off Lorn hys lyff at Wallace aft,
On Makfadzane with worthy men he paft,
He grantyt hym to put yaim all to dede,
Yai left nane quyk, fyne brocht Wallace hys hed,
Apon a fper throuchout ye feild it bar. 865
Ye Lord Cambell yan hynt it by ye har,
Heich in Cragmor he maid it for to ftand,
Steild on a ftayne for honour off Irland.
Ye bleffit men qat war off Scotland born,
Fownde at hys faith Wallace gert yaim be fuorn, 870
Reftoryt yaim to yair landis but lefs,
He leit fla nayne yat wald cum till hys pefs.
Eftir yis deid in Lorn fyne couth he fayr,
Rewllyt ye land had beyne in mekill cayr.
In Archatan a cunfaill he gert cry, 875
Quhar mony man focht till hys fenzory.
All Lorn he gaiff to Dunkan yat was wycht,
And bad hym hald Scotland with ye rycht,
And yow fall weill bruk yis in heretage;
Yi brodyrs fone at London has grettar wage, 880

Zeit

Zeit will he cum, he fall hys lands haiff,
I wald tyne nayne yat rychtwyfnes mycht faiff.
Mony trew Scott to Wallace couth perfew,
At Archatan fra feill ftrenthis yai drew.
A gud knycht come, and with hym men fexte, 885
He had beyn oft in mony ftrang jeperte
With Inglifmen and fonzeid nocht a deill,
Ay fra yair faith he fendyt hym full weill,
Kepyt hym fre yocht King Edwarde had fuorn,
Schyr Jhon Ramfay, yat rychtwyfs ayr was borne
Off Ouchtir-houfs, and oyir lands, was lord,
And fchirreff als, as my buk will record,
Off nobill blud, and als haill anceftre,
Contenyt weill with worthy chewalre;
Intill Strathern yat lang tyme he had beyne, 895
At gret debait agaynys hys enemyfs keyne,
Rycht wychtly wan hys lewing into wer;
Till hym and hys Sothroune did mekill der;
Weill efchewit, and fufferyt gret diftrefs;
Hys fone was callyt ye flour off courtlynefs, 900
As witnes weill into yat fchort tretty;
Eftir ye Bruce, quha reds in yat ftory,
He rewllyt weill bath into wer and pefs,
Alexander Ramfay to nayme he hecht but lefs;
Quhen it was wer till armes he hym keft, 905
Undir ye croune he was ane off ye beft;
In tyme off pefs till courtlynes he zeid,
Bot to gentrice he tuk no oyir heid.
Quhat gentill man had nocht with Ramfay beyne;
Off courtlynes yai count hym nocht a preyne; 910
                                              Fredome

Fredome and treuth he had as men would afs,
Sen he began na bettyr fquier was;
Roxburch hauld he wan full manfully,
Syne held it lang quhill tratowris trefonably
Caufit hys dede, I can nocht tell yow how, 915
Off fic things I will ga by as now;
I haiff had blayme to fay ye futhfaftnes,.
Yarfor I will bot lychtly ryn yat cace;
Bot it be thing yat playnly flandrit is,
For fic I trew yai fuld deyme me na mifs. 920
Off gud Alexandir as now I fpek no mar,
Hys fadyr come, as I tald off befor,
Wallace off hym rycht full gud comfort hais,
For weill he coud do gret harmyng till hys fais;
In wer he was rycht mekill for to pryfs, 925
Befy and trew, bath fobyr, wycht and wyfs.
A gud prelat als to Archatan focht,
Off hys lordfchip as yan he bruikyt nocht;
Yis worthi clerk, cummyn off hys lynage,
Off Synclar blud, nocht forty zer off age, 930
Chofyne he was, be ye Papis confent,
Off Dunkell Lord, hym maid with gud entent.
Bot Inglifmen, yat Scotland gryppit all,
Off benyfice yai leit hym bruk bot fmall.
Quhen he faw weill yarfor he mycht not mute, 935
To faiff hys lyff thre zers he duelt in But,
Leifyde as he mycht, and kepyt ay gud part,
Undir faifte of Jamys yan Lord Stewart,
Till gud Wallace, quilk Scotland wan with payne,
Reftord yis Lord till hys leffyng agayne; 940

And

And mony ma, yat lang had beyne outthrawin,
Wallace yaim put rycht wyfly to yair awne.
Ye fmall oft als, ye quhilk I fpak off ayr,
Into ye hycht yat Wallace lewyt yar,
Come to ye feild quhar Makfadzane had beyne, 945
Tuk at was left, bathe weid and wappynys fcheyne,
Throw Lorn fyne paft als gudly as yai can,
Off yair nowmyr yai had nocht loft a man;
On ye fyft day yai wan till Archatan,
Quhar Wallace baid with gud men mony ane. 950
He welcummyt yaim apon a gudly wyfs,
And faid yai war rycht mekill for to pryfs,
And trew Scotts he honourit into wer,
Gaiff yat he wan hymfelff kepyt no ger.
Quhen Wallace wald na langar foiorn yar, 955
Fra Archattan throw out ye land yai far,
Towart Dunkell with gud men off renoun,
Hys maift thocht yan was haill on Santt Jhoneftoun.
He callyt Ramfay, yat gud knycht off gret waill,
Sadly awyfyt befoucht hym off confaill; 960
Yar I haiff beyne, and loft men apon chance,
Bot ay for ane we gert ten off yaim de,
And zeit me think yat is no mends to me,
I wald affay, off yis land or we gang,
And lat yaim witt yai occupy her with wrang. 965
Yan Ramfay faid, yat towne yai may nocht kepe,
Ye wallis ar laych, fuppofs ye dyk be depe,
Ze haiff enewch, yat fall yaim cummyr fa,
Fyll up ye dyk, yat we may playnly ga
In haill battaill, a thowfand our at anys, 970
Fra

Fra yis power yai fall nocht hald yon wanys.
Wallace was glaid yat he sic comfort maid,
Furth talkand yus on to Dunkell yai raid.
Four dayis yar yai lugyt with plefance,
Quhill tyme yai had forfeyne yair ordinance. 975
Ramfay gert bygg ftrang beftialls off tre,
Be gud wrychts ye beft in yat cuntre;
Quhan yai war wrocht, betaucht yaim men to leid
Ye wattir doun, quhill yai come to yat fteid.
Schyr Jhon Ramfay rycht gudly was yair gyd, 980
Rewllyt yaim weill at hys will for to byd.
Ye gret oft yan about ye willage paft,
With crd and ftayne yai fillyt dyks faft,
Flaiks yai laid on ternyr lang and wycht,
A rowme paffage to ye wallis yaim dycht; 985
Feill beftialls rycht ftarkly up yai raifs,
Gud men off armys fone till affailʒe gais.
Schyr Jhone ye Grayme, and Ramfay yat was wycht,
Ye Turat Bryg fegyt with all yair mycht;
And Wallace felff at mydfid off ye toune, 990
With men off armys yai was to bargane bown.
Ye Sothroune men maid gret defens yat tyd,
With artailʒe, yat felloune was to byd,
With awblafters gaynʒe, and ftanys faft,
And hand gunnys rycht brymly out yai caft; 995
Punʒeid with fpers men off armys fcheyne.
Ye worthi Scotts, yat cruell war and keyne,
At hand ftraikis fra yai togydder met,
With Sothroune blud yair wappynys fone yai wett:
Zett Inglifmen, yat worthy war in wer, 1000

Into

Into ye ſtour rycht bauldly can yaim ber,
Bot all for nocht awailzeid yaim yat deid,
Ye Scotts throw force apon yaim in yai zaid;
A thouſand men our wallis zeid haſtely,
Into ye toune raiſs hidewyſs noyis and cry,   1005
Ramſay and Grayme ye turat zeitt has wown,
And entrit in, quhar gret ſtryff has begowne.
A trew ſquier, quhilk Reven hecht be nayme,
Come to ye ſalt with gud Schyr Jhon ye Grayme,
Threty with hym off men yat prowit weill,   1010
Amang yair fayis with wappynys ſtiff off ſteill.
Quhen at ye Scotts ſemblyt on ayir ſyd,
Na Sothroune was yat mycht yair dynt abyd.
Twa thouſand ſone was fulzied undirfeit,
Off Sothroune blud lay ſtekyt in ye ſtreit.   1015
Schyr Jhon Sewart ſaw weill ye town was ſtynt,
Tuk hym to flycht, and wald na langar ſtynt,
In a lycht barge, and with hym men ſexte,
Ye wattir doun, ſocht ſuccour at Dunde.
Wallace baid ſtill quhill ye ferd day at morn,   1020
And left nayne yar yat war off Ingland born.
Ryches yai gat off gold and oyir gud,
Plenyſt ye towne agayne with Scotts blud;
Ruwan he left yair Captayne for to be,
In heretage gaiff hym office to fee   1025
Off all Strathern, and ſchirreff off ye toun,
Syne in ye north gud Wallace maid hym boun.
In Abyrdeyn he gert a conſaill cry,
Trew Scotts men ſuld ſemble haſtely.
Till Cowper he raid to weſy yat Abbay,   1030
Ye

Ye Inglis Abbot fra ynce was fled away.
Bifchop Synclar, without langar abaid,
Met yaim at Glammyfs, fyne furth with yaim he raid.
Intill Breichyn yai lugyt all yat nycht,
Syne on ye morn Wallace gert graith yaim rycht, 1035
Difplayed on breid ye Banir off Scotland,
In gud aray, with nobill men at hand;
Gert playnly cry yat fawfte fuld be nayne
Off Sotheroune blud quhar yai mycht be ourtayn
In playn battaill throchout ye Mernyfs yai rid. 1040
Ye Inglifmen at durft yaim nocht abid
Befor ye oft full ferdly furth yai fle
Till Dunottar a fwak within ye fe
Na ferrar yai mycht wyn out off ye land
Yai femblit yar quhill yai war four thoufand 1045
To ye kyrk rane, wend girth for till haiff tayne,
Ye laiff ramaynd apon ye rock off ftayne.
Ye Byfchop yan began tretty to ma,
Yair lyffs to get out off ye land to ga.
Bot yai war rad, and durft nocht weyll affy; 1050
Wallace in fyr gert fet all haiftely,
Brynt up ye kyrk, and all yat was yarin,
Atour ye rock ye laiff ran with gret dyn;
Sum hang on craggs rycht dulfully to de,
Sum lap, fum fell, fum flotyret in ye fe, 1055
Na Sothroune on lyff was lewyt in yat hauld,
And yaim within yai brynt in powdir cauld.
Quhen yis was doyn, feill fell on kneis doun,
At ye Byfchop afkyt abfolutioun.
Yan Wallace lewch, faid, I forgiff yow all, 1060

Ar

Ar ze wer men rapents for fa fmall?
Yai rewid nocht us in to ye toune off Ayr,
Owr trew Barrowns quhen yat yai hangyt yar.
Till Abyrdeyn yan haiftely yai pafs,
Quhar Inglifmen befyly flittand was. 1065
Ane hundreth fchippis, yat ruther bur and ayr,
To turfs yair gud, in hawyn was lyand yar:
Bot Wallace oft come on yaim fodeynlye,
Yar chapyt nane off all yat gret menzhe;
Bot feill ferwands in yaim lewyt nane, 1070
At ane eb fe ye Scotts is on yaim gayne,
Tuk out ye ger, fyne fet ye fchippis in fyr,
Ye men on land yai bertynyt bayne and lyr;
Zeid nane away bot preifts, wiffis and barnys,
Maid yai debait, yai chapyt nocht but harmys. 1075
Into Bowchane Wallace maid hym to ryd,
Quhar Lord Bewmound was ordand for to byd,
Erle he was maid off bot fchort tyme befor,
He brukit nocht for all hys buftous fchor.
Quhen he wyft weill yat Wallace cummand was, 1080
He left ye land, and couth to Slanys pafs,
And fyne be fchipin Ingland fled agayne.
Wallace raid throw ye north land into playne.
At Crummade feill Inglifmen yai flew.
Ye worthi Scotts till hym yus couth perfew. 1085
Raturnd agayne, and come till Abyrdeyn,
With hys blyth oft, apon ye Lammefs ewyn,
Stablyt ye land, as hym thocht beft fuld be,
Syne with ane oft he paffit to Dunde,
Gert fet a fege about ye caftell ftrang. 1090

VOL. II. D I leyff

I leyff yaim yar, and foryir we will gang.
Schyr Amar Wallang haiftit hym full faft,
Intill Ingland, with hys haill houfhald paft;
Bothwell he left, was Murrayis heretage,
And tuk hym yan bot to King Edwards wage. 1095
Yus hys awne land forfuk for euirmar,
Off Wallace deid gret tithands tald he yar.
Als Inglifmen fair murnyt in yair mude,
Had loffyt her bath lyff, landis and gud.
Edward as yan couth nocht in Scotland fair, 1100
Bot Kertymgame, yat was hys Treforair,
With hym a lord, yan Erle was off Waran,
He chargyt yaim, with nowmris mony ane,
Rycht weill befeyn, in Scotland for to ryd.
At Stirlyng ftill he ordand yaim to byd, 1105
Quhill he mycht cum with ordinance off Ingland,
Scotland agayne he thocht to tak in hand.
Yis oft paft furth, and had bot litill dreid,
Ye Erle Patrick refawit yaim at Tweid,
Malice he had at gud Wallace befor, 1110
Lang tyme by paft, and yan increffyt mor:
Bot throch a cafs, yat hapnyt off hys wyff,
Dunbar fche held from hym into yair ftryff,
Throuch ye fupple off Wallace into playne,
Bot he be mayne gat hys caftell agayne 1115
Lang tyme or yan, and zeit he couth nocht cefs,
Agayne Wallace he prowit in mony prefs,
With Inglifmen, fuppleit at hys mycht,
Contrar Scotland yai wrocht full gret unrycht.
Yair muftir yan was awful for to fe, 1120
Off

Off fechtand men thoufands yai war fexte
To Stirling paft, or yai likit to byd,
To Erle Malcom a fege yai laid yat tyd,
And thocht to kep ye cummaund off yair King;
Bot gud Wallace wrocht for ane oyir thing.   1125
Dunde he left, and maid a gud Chyftane,
With twa thoufand, to kepe yat houfs off ftayne,
Off Angwyfs men, and duellars off Dunde;
Ye famyn nycht till Santt Jhonftoun went he.
Apon ye morn to Schirreff-mur he raid,   1130
And yar a quhill, in gud aray, yai baid.
Schyr Jhon ye Grayme, and Ramfay yat was wycht,
He faid to yaim, yis is my purpofs rycht,
Our mekill it is to proffer yaim battaill,
Apon a playne feild, bot we haiff fum awaill.   1135
Schyr Jhon ye Grayme faid we haiff undirtane,
With lefs power, fic thing yat weill is gayn.
Yan Wallace faid, quhar fic thing cummys off neid,
We fuld thank God yat makis us for to fpeid,
Bot ner ye Bryg my purpofs is to be,   1140
And wyrk for yaim fum futtell jeperte.
Ramfay anfuerd, ye Bryg we may keip weill,
Off way about Sothroune has litill feill.
Wallace fent Jop ye battaill for to fet,
Ye Twefday next to fecht withoutyn let.   1145
On Sattirday on to ye Bryg yai raid,
Off gud playne burd was weill and junctly maid;
Gert wachis wait, yat nane fuld fra yaim pafs.
A wricht he tuk, ye futtelaft at yar was,
And ordand hym to faw ye burd in twa,   1150

Be ye mid ftreit, yat nane mycht our it ga;
On charnaill bands nald it full faft and fone,
Syne fyld with clay as na thing had beyne done.
Ye toyir end he ordand for to be,
How it fuld ftand on thre rowars off tre, 1155
Quhen ane war out, yat ye laiff dounc fuld fall;
Hymfelf undyr he ordand yar with all,
Bownd on ye treft in a credill to fit,
To loufs ye pyne quhen Wallace leit hym witt
Bot with a horn, quhen it was tyme to be; 1160
In all ye oft fuld na man blaw bot he.
Ye day approchit off ye gret battaill,
Ye Iniflmen for power wald nocht faill,
Ay fex yai war agayne ane off Wallace,
Fyfte thoufand maid yaim to battaill place; 1165
Ye ramaynand baid at ye caftell ftill,
Baith feild and houfs yai thocht to tak at will.
Ye worthi Scotts, apon ye toyir fyd,
Ye playne feild tuk, on fute maid yaim to byd.
Hew Kyrtyngayme ye wantgard leds he, 1170
With twenty thoufand off likly men to fe.
Threty thoufand the Erle off Waran had,
Bot he did yan as ye wyffman hym bad;
All ye fyrft oft befor hym our was fend.
Sum Scotts men, yat weill ye mattir kend, 1175
Bade Wallace blaw, and faid, yai war enew.
He haiftyt nocht, bot fadly couth perfew,
Quhill Warans oft thik on ye Bryg he faw,
Fra Jop ye Horn he hyntyt and couth blaw,
Sa afprely, and warned gud Jhon Wricht, 1180

Ye

Ye rowar out he ftraik with gret flycht;
Ye laiff zeid doun, quhen ye pynnys out gais.
A hidwyfs cry amang ye pepill raifs,
Bath horfs and men into ye wattir fell.
Ye hardy Scotts, yat wald na langar duell,   1185
Set on ye laiff with ftrakis fad and far,
Off yaim yarour, as yan fowerit yai war.
At ye forbreft yai prowit hardely,
Wallace and Grayme, Boid, Ramfay, and Lundy,
All in ye ftour faft fechtand face to face.   1190
Ye Sothroune oft bak rerit off yat place
At yai fyrft tuk, fyffe akyr breid and mar.
Wallace on fute a gret fcharp fper he bar,
Amang ye thikeft off ye prefs he gais,
On Kertyngayme a ftraik chofyn he hais   1195
In ye byrnes, yat polyft was full brycht,
Ye punzeand hed ye platts perfyt rycht,
Throch ye body ftekit hym but refkew,
Derfly to dede yat Chyftane was adew;
Baith man and horfs at yat ftraik he bar doun.   1200
Ye Inglis oft, quhill war in battaill bown,
Comfort yai loft quhen yair Chyftayne was flayne,
And mony ane to fle began in playne;
Zeit worthi men baid ftill into ye fted,
Quhill ten thoufand was broucht on to yair dede. 1205
Yan fled ye laiff, and mycht no langar byd,
Succour yai focht on mony diuerfs fyd,
Sum eft, fum weft, and fum fled to ye north,
Sewyn thoufand large at anys flottryt in Forth,
Plungyt ye depe, and drownd withoutyn mercy,   1210

Nayne left on lyff off all yat feill menzhe.
Off Wallace oft na man was flayne off waill,
Bot Andrew Murray into yat ftrang battaill.
Ye fouth part faw at yar men was tynt,
As ferfly fled as fyr dois off ye flynt.   1215
Ye place yai left, Caftell, and Stirlyng toune,
Towart Dunbar in gret haift yai maid yaim boune.
Quhen Wallace oft had won yat feild throuch mycht,
Tuk up ye Bryg, and louffit gud Jhon Wricht;
On ye flears fyne folowed wondyr faft,   1220
Erle Malcom als out off ye caftell paft,
With Lenox men to ftuff ye chace gud fpeid,
Ay be ye way yai gert feill Sothroune bleid;
In ye Torwode yai gert full mony de.
Ye Erle off Waran, yat can full ferfly fle,   1225
With Corfpatrik, yat graithly was hys gyd,
On changit horfs throuchout ye land yai ryd,
Strawcht to Dunbar, bot few with yaim yai led;
Mony war flayne our fleuthfully yat fled.
Ye Scotts horfs yat had rown wondyr lang,   1230
Mony gaiff our, yat mycht na forthyr gang.
Wallace and Grayme euir togyddyr baid,
At Hathyngtoun full gret flauchtir yai maid
Off Inglifmen, quhen yair horfs tyrit had.
Quhen Ramfay come gud Wallace was full glad,   1235
With hym was Boid, and Richard off Lundy,
Thre thoufand haill was off gud chewalry,
And Adam als Wallace off Ricardtoun,
With Erle Malcom, yai fand at Hathyngtoun.
Ye Scotts men on flauchtyr toryt was,   1240
                                                    Quhill

Quhill to Dunbar ye twa Chyftanes couth pafs,
Full fitfully, for yair gret contrar cafs,
Wallace folowed till yai gat in yat place.
Off yair beft men, and Kertyngayme off renoun,
Twenty thoufand was dede but redemptioun. 1245
Befyd Beltoun Wallace raturnd agayn,
To folow mar as yan was bot in wayn.
In Hathyngtoun lugyng yai maid yat nycht,
Apon ye morn to Stirling paffit rycht.
Affumptioune day off Marye fell yis cafs, 1250
Ay lowit be our lady off hyr grace;
Conuoyar oft fche was off gud Wallace,
And helpyt hym in mony fyndry place.
Wallace in haift, fone eftir yis battaill,
A gret aith tuk off all ye Barrons haill, 1255
Yat with gud will wald cum till hys prefens;
He hecht yaim als to byd at yair defens.
Schyr Jhon Menteth was yan off Aran Lord,
Till Wallace come, and maid a playne record,
With witnes yar be hys ayth he hym band, 1260
Lawta to kepe to Wallace and Scotland.
Quha with fre will till rycht wald nocht apply,
Wallace with force punyft rygorufly;
Part put to dede, part fet in pryfone ftrang,
Gret word off hym throuch bath yir regiouns rang.
Dunde yai gat fone be a fchort trete,
Bot for yair lywes, and fled away be fe.
Inglis captaynes, yat houfs had into hand,
Left caftells fre, and fled out off ye land.
Within ten dayis eftir yis tym was gayne, 1270

Inglis

Inglis captaynes in Scotland left was nayne,
Except Berweik, and Roxburch Caftell wycht,
Zeit Wallace thocht to bryng yaim to ye rycht.
Yat tyme yar was a worthy Barroun,
To nayme he hecht gud Criftall off Cetoun,   1275
In Jedwort wode for faiffgard he had beyne,
Agayne Sothrouue full weill he couth opteyn;
In owtlaw oyfs he lewit yar but let,
Edwarde couth not fra Scotts faith hym get.
Herbottell fled fra Jedwort Caftell wycht   1280
Towart Ingland, yar Cetoun met hym rycht;
With fourty men Cryftall in bargane baid,
Agayne aucht fcor, and mekill maiftir maid,
Slew yat Captayne, and mony cruell man;
Full gret ryches in yat jornay he wan,   1285
Housfhald and gold, as yai fuld pafs away,
Ye quhilk befor yai kepyt mony day.
Jedwort yai tuk, ane Ruwan lewyt he
At Wallace will Captane off it to be.
Bauld Cetoun fyne to Lothiane made repair,   1290
In yis ftorye ze man her off hym mair,
And into Bruce quha likis for to rede,
He was with hym in mony cruell deid.
Gud Wallace yan full fadly can dewyfs,
To rewill ye land with worthi men and wyfs;   1295
Captayns he maid, and Schirreffs yat was gud,
Part off hys kyn, and off trew oyir blud.
Hys der cufyng in Edynburgh ordand he,
Ye trew Crawfurd, yat ay was full worthe,
Kepar off it, with nobill men at wage,   1300

In

In Mannuell yan he had gud heretage.
Scotland was fre, yat lang in baill had beyn,
Throw Wallace won fra our falfs enemys keyn.
Gret Gouernour in Scotland he couth ryng,
Wayttand a tyme to get hys rychtwyfs King.   1305
Fra Inglis men, yat held hym in bandoun,
Lang wrangwyfly fra hys awne rychtwyfs croun.

   EXPLICIT LIBER SEPTIMUS.
   ET INCIPIT OCTAVUS.

THE LIFE OF SIR WILLIAM WALLACE, &c.

BOOK VIII.

Wallace Drives the Earl of March out of Scotland—Defeats Corspatrick and Bruce at Spots Mure—At Lammermuire—Rewards his Followers—Ravages England—Besieges York—Takes Ramswaith—Sends a Woman to King Edward—At St Albin's—The Queen of England comes to Sue for Peace—Wallace agrees—Peace made—Lasts Three Years—Wallace goes to France.

FYWE monethis yus Scotland stud in gud rest,
 A consaill cryit, yaim thocht it was ye best,
In Sanct Jhonstoune yat it suld haldyn be,
Assemblit yar Clerk, Barown, and Bowrugie,
Bot Corspatrik wald nocht cum at yair call,   5.
Baid in Dunbar, and maid scorn at yaim all.
Yai spak off hym feill words in yat parlyment.
Yan Wallace said, will ze herto consent,
Forgyff hym fre all things yat ar by past,
Sa he will com and grant he has trespast,   10

Fra yis tyme furth kepe Lawta till our croun.
Yai grant yarto, Clerk, Burgefs, and Barroun,
With haill confent yair wrytyng till hym fend,
Rycht lawly yus to hym yai yaim commend,
Befoucht hym fayr, as a Peyr off ye land, 15
To cum and tak fum Gouernaill on hand.
Lychtly he lewch, in fcorn as it had beyne,
And faid he had fic meffage feldyn feyne,
Yat Wallace now as Gouernour fall ryng,
Her is gret faute off a gud prince or king; 20
Yat King off Kyll I can nocht undirftand,
Off hym I held neuir a fur off land;
Yat Bachiller Trowis, for fortoun fchawis hyr quhell,
Yarwith to left, it fall nocht lang be weill:
Bot to yow lords, and ze will undirftand, 25
I mak yow wyfs, I aw to mak na band,
Als fre I am in yis regioun to ryng,
Lord off myn awne, as euyr was prince or king;
In Ingland als gret part off land I haiff,
Mawrent yaroff yar will no man me craiff. 30
Quhat will yow mar, I warn zow I am fre,
For your fomounds ze get na mair off me.
Till Sanct Jhonftoune yis wryt he fend agayne,
Befor ye lords was manifeft and playne,
Quhen Wallace herd ye Erle fic anfuer mais, 35
A gret hate ire throw curage yan he tais;
For weill he wyft yar fuld be bot a king
Off yis regioun, at anys for to ryng;
A King off Kyll, for yat he callit Wallace.
Lords, he faid, yis an uncouth cace, 40
Be

Be he fuffyryt, we haiff war yan it was;
Yus raifs he up, and maid hym for to pafs;
God has us tholyt to do fo for ye laiff,
In lyff or dede in faith hym fall we haiff,
Or ger hym grant quhom he holds for hys lord, 45
Or ellis war fchapyn in ftory to racord;
I wow to God with eyfs he fall nocht be
Into yis realm, bot ane off us fall de,
Lefs yan he cum, and knaw hys rychtwyfs king,
In yis regioun weille bathe we fall nocht ryng; 50
Hys lychtly fcorn he fall rapent full for,
Bot power faill, or I fall end yarfor,
Sen in yis erd is ordand me no reft,
Now God be juge ye rycht he kennys beft.
At yat cunfaill langar he taryt nocht, 55
With twa hundreth fra Santt Jhohftonne he focht;
To ye cunfaill maid inftans or he zeid,
Yai fuld conteyn, and off hym haiff na dreid,
I am bot ane, and for gud caufs I ga.
Towart kyngorn ye gayneft way yai ta; 60
Apon ye morn atour Forth fouth yai paft,
On yis wyage yai haiftit wondyr faft.
Robert Laudir at Muffilburgh met Wallace,
Fra Inglifmen he kepyt weill hys place,
South nane hym trete, knycht, fquier nor lord, 65
With King Edwarde to be at ane accord;
On Erle Patrick to pafs he was full glaid,
Sum faid befor ye bafs he wald haiff haid.
Gud men als come with Cryftall off Cetoune;
Yan Wallace was four hundreth off renoune. 70

A

A fqueir Lyll, yat weill yat cuntre knew,
With twentye men to Wallace couth perfew,
Befyd Lintoun, and to yaim tald he yan,
Ye Erle Patrik with mony likly man,
At Coburns peth he had hys gaderyng maid,   75
And to Dunbar wald cum withoutyn baid.
Yan Lawder faid, it war ye beft think me,
Fafter to pafs, in Dunbar or he be.
Wallace anfuerd, we may at layfar ryd,
With zone power he thinkis bargane to byd;   80
And off a thing ze fall weill undirftand
A hardyar lord is nocht into Scotland;
Mycht he be maid trew ftedfaft till a king,
Be wit and force he can do mekill thing:
Bot wilfully he likis to tyne hymfell.   85
Yus raid yai furth, and wald na langar duell,
Be eft Dunbar, quhar men hym tald on cace,
Quhow Erle Patrik was warnyt off Wallace,
Ner Ennerweik chefyt a feild at waill,
With nyne hundreth off likly men to waill.   90
Four hundreth was with Wallace in ye rycht,
And fone onon approchit to yair fycht.
Gret fawte yar was of gud trety betweyn,
To mak concord, and yat full fone was feyn.
Without raherfs off actioun in yat tyd,   95
On ayir pait togyddir faft yai ryd.
Ye ftour was ftrang, and wondyr peralous,
Contenyt lang with deds chewalrous;
Mony yar deit of cruell Scotts blud:
Off yis trety ye mater is nocht gud,   100

Yarfor I cefs to tell ye deftructioune,
Pete it was and all off a natioune.
Bot Erle Patrik ye feild left at ye laft,
Rycht few with hym to Coburns peth yai paft,
Agrewit far yat hys men yus war tynt.   105
Was raturnd, and wald na langar ftynt,
Towart Dunbar, quhar futh faft men hym tald,
Na purweance was left into yat hald,
Nor men off fens, all had beyne with yair lord.
Quhen Wallace hard ye fekyr trew record,   110
Dunbar he tuk all haill at hys bandoune,
Gaiff it to kepe to Cryftell off Cetoune,
Quhilk ftuffyt it weill with men and gud wictaill.
Apon ye morn, Wallace yat wald nocht faill,
With thre hundreth, to Coburns peth he focht: 115
Erle Patrik ufchyt, for byd hym wald he nocht.
Sone to ye Park Wallace a range has fet;
Till Bonkill wode Corfpatrik fled but let,
And out off it till Noram paffit he.
Quhen Wallace faw it mycht na bettir be,   120
Till Caudftreym went and lugyt hym on Tweid.
Erle Patrik yan, in all haift can hym fpeid,
And paffit by or Wallace power raifs,
Without reftyng in Atryk forreft gais.
Wallace folowed, bot he wald nocht affaill,   125
A range to mak as yan it mycht not waill;
Our few he had, ye ftrenth was thik and ftrang,
Sewyn myill on breid, and yarto twyfs fa lang.
Intill Corkhelm Erle Patrik leiffit at reft.
For mar power Wallace paft in ye weft.   130

Erle

Erle Patrik yan hym graithit haftelye,
In Ingland paft to get hym yar fupplye;
Out throuch ye land rycht erneftfully couth pafs,
Tald Anton Beik yat Wallace cnmmand was.
Wallace hym put out off Glafkow befor,   135
And flew Perfye yair malice was ye mor.
Ye Byfchope Beik gert fone power ryfs,
Northummyrland upon ane awfull wyfs.
Yan ordand Bruce in Scotland for to pafs,
To wyn hys awne, bot ill defawit he was;   140
Yai gart hym trew yat Wallace was rabell,
And thoucht to tak ye kynryk to hym fell.
Full falfs yai war, and cuir zeit has beyne,
Lawta and treuth was ay in Wallace feyne;
To fend ye rycht all yat he tuk on hand,   145
And thocht to bryng ye Bruce fre till hys land.
Off yis mater as now I tary nocht.
With ftrang power Sothroune togydder focht;
Fra Oufs wattir affemblit haill to Tweid.
Yair land oft was threty thoufand in deid.   150
Off Tynnys mouth fend fchippis be ye fe,
To kep Dunbar at nayne fuld yaim fupple.
Erle Patrik with twenty thoufand but let,
Befor Dunbar a ftalwart fege he fet.
Ye Byfchope Beik and Robert Bruce baid ftill, 155
With ten thoufand, at Noram at yair will.
Wallace be yis, yat faft was laubourand,
In Lothyane com with gud men fyfe thoufand,
Rycht weill befeyn, all into armyfs brycht,
Thocht to refkew ye Cetoun bauld and brycht. 160

Undyr zheftyr yat fyrft nycht lugit he;
Hay com till hym with a gud chewalre,
In Duns foreft all yat tyme he had beyne,
Ye cummyng yar off Sothroune he had feyne;
Fyftye he had off befy men in wer,   165
Yai tald Wallace off Patriks gret affer.
Yai faid, forfuth, and ze mycht hym ourfet,
Power agayne rycht fone he mycht not get,
My cunfaill is, yat we giff hym battaill.
He thankyt hym off comfort and confaill,   170
And faid, freynd Hay, in yis caufs yat I wend,
Sa yat we wyn, I rek nocht for till end,
Rycht futh it is yat anys we mon de,
Into ye rycht quha fuld in terrour be.
Erle Patrik yan a meffynger gert pafs,   175
Tald Anton Beik yat Wallace cummand was.
Off yis tithings ye Byfchope was full glaid,
Amends off hym full fayne he wald haiff haid.
Bot mar prolong throuch Lammer-muir yai raid,
Ner ye Spot-Mur in bufchement ftill he baid,   180
As Erle Patrik ordand yaim for to be.
Wallace off Beik unwarnyt yan was he;
Zeit he befor was nocht haifty in deid,
Bot yan he put bathe hym and hys in dreid.
Apon fwyft horfs fcurrours paft betweyn.   185
Ye cummyng yan off Erle Patrik was feyn,
Ye houfs he left, and to ye mur is gayne,
A playne feild yar with hys oft he has tayn.
Gud Cetoun fyne ufchet with few menzhe,
Part off hys men intill Dunbar left he,   190

To

To Wallace raid was on ye rychtwyſs ſyd;
In gud aray to ye Spot-Mur yai ryd.
Sum Scotts dred, ye Erle ſa mony was,
Twentye thouſand agayne ſa few, to paſs.
Quhen Jop perſauit, he bad Wallace ſuld byd.   195
Tyne nocht yir men, but to ſum ſtrenth ze ryd,
And I ſall paſs to get yow power mar,
Yir ar our gud yus lychtly for to war.
Yan Wallace ſaid, in trewth I will nocht fle,
For four off hys, ay ane quhill I may be;   200
We ar our ner ſic purpoſs for to tak,
A danger chace yai mycht apon us mak;
Her is twenty, with yis power, to day,
Wald hym aſſay, ſuppoſs I war away;
Mony yai ar, for Godds luff be we ſtrang,   205
Yon Sothroune folk in ſtour will nocht byd lang.
Ye brym battaill braithly on ayir ſyd.
Gret rerd yar raiſs all ſammyn quhar yai ryd.
Ye ſayr ſembly, quhen yai togydder met,
Feill ſtraks yar ſadly on ayir ſet,   210
Punzeand ſpers throuch platts perfit faſt;
Mony off horſs to ye ground doun yai caſt,
Saidlys yai teym off horſs, bot maiſtirs, yar,
Off ye ſouth ſyd fyffe thouſand doun yai bar.
Gud Wallace oſt ye formaſt cumbraid ſa,   215
Quhill ye laiff was in will away to ga.
Erle Patrik baid, ſa cruell off entent,
At all hys oſt tuk off hym hardyment:
Agayne Wallace in mony ſtour was he.
Wallace knew weill, yat hys men wald nocht fle   220

For na power yat lyffand was in lyff,
Quhill yai in heill mycht ay be ane for fyffe.
In yat gret ftryff mony was handlyt halt;
Ye feill dynts, ye cruell hard debait,
Ye fers ftykyng maid mony grewows wound,   225
Upon ye erd ye blud did till abound.
All Wallace oft intill a cumpaifs baid,
Quhar fa yai turnd full gret flauchtyr yai maid.
Wallace and Grayme, and Ramfay full worthy,
Ye Bauld Cetoun, and Richard off Lundy,   230
Adam als Wallace off Ricardtoun,
Bathe Hay and Lyll, with gud men off renoun,
Boyd, Bercla, Byrd, and Lawdar yat was wycht,
Feill Inglifmen derfly to ded yai dycht.
Bot Erle Patrik full ferfly faucht agayn,   235
Throuch hys awne hand he put mony to payn.
Our men on hym thrang forthwart into thra,
Maid throuch hys oft feill floppis to and fra.
Ye Inglifmen began playnlye to fle;
Yan Byfchope Beik full fodeynly yai fe,   240
And Robert Bruce, contrar hys natiff men;
Wallace was wa, fra tyme he couth hym ken.
Off Bruces deid he was agrewit far mar,
Yan all ye laiff yat day at femblit yar.
Ye gret bufchement at anys brak on breid,   245
Ten thoufand haill yat douchty war in deid.
Ye flears yan with Erle Patrik relefd,
To fecht agayn, quhar mony war mifcheifd.
Quhen Wallace knew ye bufchement brokyn was,
Out off ye feild on horfs yai thocht to pafs: 250
Bot

Bot he faw weill hys oft fownd in yair weid,
He thoucht to fray ye formaft as yai zeid.
Ye new cummyn oft befor yaim femblit yar,
On ayir fyde. With ftrakis fad and far,
Ye worthy Scotts fa ferfly faucht agayne, 255
Off Antonys men rycht mony haiff yai flayne:
Bot yat terand fo ufyt was in wer,
On Wallace oft yai did full mekill der.
And ye bauld Bruce fa cruelly wrocht he,
Throuch ftrenth off hand feill Scots he gert de. 260
To refift Bruce Wallace hym preffit faft,
Bot Inglifmen fa thik betwixt yaim paft;
And Erle Patrik, in all ye haift he moucht,
Throuchout ye ftour to Wallace fone he focht;
On ye the pefs a felloune ftrak hym gaiff, 265
Herwit ye plait with hys fcharp groundyn claiff,
Throuch all ye ftuff and woundyt hym fum deill:
Bot Wallace thocht he fuld be wengyt weill,
Folowed on hym and a ftraik etlyt faft,
Yan ane Mawthland raklefs betwix yaim paft; 270
Apon ye hed gud Wallace has hym tane,
Throch hat and brawn in fondyr byrft ye bane,
Deid at yat ftraik donn to ye ground hym drawe.
Yus Wallace was diffuiryt fra ye lawe
Off hys gud men, amang yaim hym allane. 275
About hym focht till enymyfs mony ane,
Stekit hys horfs, to ground behufid hym lycht,
To fend hymfelff, as wifely as he mycht.
Ye worthi Scotts, yat mycht na langar hyd,
With fair harts out off ye feild yai ryd. 280

With

With yaim in feyr yai wend Wallace had beyne,
On fute he was amang hys enymyſs keyne;
Gud rowme he maid about hym into breid;
With hys gud ſuerd yat helpyt hym in neid.
Was nane ſa ſtrang, yat gat off hym a ſtrak,   285.
Eftir agayne maid neuir a Scott to waik.
Erle Patrik yan, yat had gret craft in wer,
With ſpers ordand gud Wallace doun to ber;
Anew yai tuk was haill into ye feild,
Till hym yai zeid, thocht he ſuld haiff no beild,   290.
On ayir ſyde faſt poyntand at hys ger;
He hewid off hedys, and wyſly coud hym wer.
Ye worthi Scotts off yis full litill wyſt,
Socht to gud Grayme quhen yai yar chyftayne myſt.
Lauder, and Lyll, and Hay, yat was full wycht,   295
And bauld Ramſay, quhilk was a worthi knycht,
Lundy, and Boid, and Cryſtell off Cetoun,
With fyffe hundreth, yat war in bargane boun,
Hym to reſkew full rudly in yai raid,
About Wallace a large rowme yai maid.   300
Ye Byſchop Beik was braithly born till erd,
At ye reſkew yar was a glamrous rerd;
Or he gat up feill Sothroune yai ſlew.
Out off ye preſs Wallace yai couth reſkew,
Sone horſſit hym apon a courſour wycht,   305
Towart a ſtrenth rydis in all yair mycht,
Rycht wyſly fled, reſkewand mony ma.
Ye Erle Patrik to ſtuff ye chace began;
On ye flears litill harm yan he wrocht.
Gud Wallace folk away togyddyr ſocht;   310

Yir

Yir fyffe hundreth, ye quhilk I fpak off ayr,
Sa awfully abaundownd yaim fo far,
Na folowar durft out fra hys falow ga,
Ye gud flears fic raturnyng yai ma.
Four thoufand haill had tane ye ftrenth befor 315
Off Wallace oft, hys cumfort was ye mor,
Off Glafhadane yat foreft thoucht to hauld.
Erle Patrik turnd, yocht he was neuer fa bauld,
Agayne to Beik, quhen chapyt was Wallace,
Curffand fortoun off hys myfchanfyt cace. 320
Ye feild he wan, and fewyn thoufand yai loft,
Dede on yat day, for all ye Byfchoppis boft.
Off Wallace men fyffe hundreth war flayne I gefs,
Bot na Chyftayne, hys murnyng was ye lefs.
Ner ewyn it was, bot Beik wald nocht abyde, 325
In Lammarmur yai trawentyt yat tyde,
Yair lugyng tuk quhar hym thocht maift awaill,
For weill he trowit ye Scotts wald affaill.
Apon ye feild, quhar yai gaiff battaill laft,
Ye contre men to Wallace gadryt faft. 330
Off Edynburch, wycht Crawfurd yat was wycht,
Thre hundreth come intill yar armour brycht.
Till Wallace raid, be hys lugeyng was tayne.
Fra Tawydaill come gud men mony ane,
Out off Jedwart, with Ruwane, at yat tyd, 335
Togyddyr focht fra mony diuerfs fyd.
Schyr Wilzam Lang yat lord was off Douglace,
With hym four fcor yat nycht come to Wallace.
Twenty hundreth off new men met yat nycht,
Apon yair fais to weng yaim at yair mycht; 340
At

At ye fyrſt feild yir gud men had not beyn.
Wallace wachis yair aduerſouris had ſeyn,
Into quhat wyſs yai had yair lugyng maid.
Wallace bownyt eftir ſupper, but baid,
In Lammarmur yai paſſit ha:ſtely ; 345
Sone till aray zeid yis gud chewalry.
Wallace yaim maid ik twa parts to be ;
Schyr Jhon ye Grayme and Cetoun ordand he,
Lawdir and Hay, with thre thouſand to ryde ;
Hymſelff ye laiff tuk wyſly for to gyde, 350
With hym Lundy, bathe Ramſay and Douglace,
Berkla and Boyd, and Adam gud Wallace.
Be yis ye day approchit wondyr ner,
And bricht Titan in preſens can apper.
Ye Scotts oft ſone ſemblyt into ſycht 355
Off yair enemyſs, yat war nocht redy dycht ;
Out off aray feill off ye Suthroune was,
Rycht awfully Wallace can on yaim paſs.
At yis entray ye Scotts ſo weill yaim bar,
Feill off yair fayis to dede was bertnyt yar. 360
Redleſs yai raiſs, and mony fled away,
Sum on ye ground war ſmoryt quhar yai lay,
Gret noyis and cry was raiſſit yaim amang.
Gud Grayme come in, yat ſtalwart was and ſtrang.
For Wallace men war weill togyddyr met, 365
On ye ſouth part ſa awfully yai ſet,
In contrar yaim ye frayit folk mycht not ſtand ;
At anys yar fled off Sothroune fyffe thouſand.
Ye worthi Scotts wrocht apon ſic wyſs,
Jop ſaid hymſelff, yai war mekill to pryſs. 370

Zeit

Zeit Byschope Beik, yat felloune tyrand strang.
Baid in ye stour rycht awfully and lang.
A Knycht Skelton, yat cruell was and keyn,
Befor hym stud intill hys armour scheyn,
To fend hys lord full worthely he wrocht. 375
Lundy hym saw, and sadly on hym socht,
With hys gud suerd an awkwart straik hym gaiff,
Throuch pesan stuff hys crag in sondyr draiff;
Quhar off ye laiff astonist in yat sted,
Ye bauld Skelton off Lundies hand is dede. 380
Yan fled yai all, and mycht na langar byd;
Patrik and Beik away with Bruce yai ryd.
Fyffe thousand held on till a slop away
Till Noram Housè, in all ye haist yai may.
Our men folowed, yat worthi war and wycht, 385
Mony fiears dersly to dede yai dycht.
Ye thre lords on to ye Castell socht,
Full feill yai left, yat was off Ingland brocht.
At yis jornay twentye thousand yai tynt,
Drownyt and slayn be sper and suerds dynt. 390
Ye Scotts at Tweid haistit yaim sa fast,
Feill Sothroune men into wrang furds past.
Wallace raturnd in Noram quhen yai war;
For worthi Bruce hys hart was wondyr sar,
He had leuer haiff had hym at hys large, 395
Fre till our croune, yan off fyne gold to carge,
Mar yan in Troy was fund at Grekis wan.
Wallace yan passit, with mony awfull man,
On Patrikis land, and waistyt wondyr fast,
Tuk out guds, and placis doun yai cast; 400

Hys

Hys fteds, fewyn yat mete hamys was cauld,
Wallace gert brek yai burly byggings bauld,
Bathe in ye Merfs, and als in Lothiane,
Except Dunbar, ftandand he lewyt nane.
Till Edynburgh, apon ye auchtand day; 405
Apon ye morn, Wallace without delay
Till Pert he paffit, quhar ye cunfaill was fet,
To ye barrowns he fchawit withoutyn let,
How hys gret wow rycht weill efchewyt was;
Till a maifter he gert Erle Patrik pafs, 410
Becaufs he faid off Scotland he held nocht,
Till King Edwarde, to get fupple, he focht.
Ye lords was blyth, and welcummyt weill Wallace,
Thankand gret God off yis fayr happy chafs.
Wallace tuk ftate to gowern all Scotland, 415
Ye barnage haill maid hym ane oppyn band.
Yan delt he land till gud men hym about,
For Scotlands rycht had fett yair lyff in dout.
Stantoun he gaiff to Lawder in hys wage,
Ye Knycht Wallang aucht it in heretage. 420
Yan Brygeane Cruk he gaiff Lyll yat was wycht;
Till Scrymgeour als full gud reward he dycht.
Syne Wallace, toun, and oyir landis yartill,
To worthi men he delt with nobill will.
To hys awne kyn heretage nane gaiff he, 425
Bot office haill, at ilk man mycht fe,
For cowatice yar couth na wycht hym blayme;
He baid reward quhill ye King fuld eum hayme;
Off all he did, he thoucht to byd ye law
Befor hys King, maifter quhen he hym faw. 430

Scotland

Scotland was blyth, in dolour had beyne lang,
In ilka part to gud labour yai gang.
Be yis ye tyme off October was paft,
Ner Nouembir approchyt wondyr faft.
Tithands yan come, King Edwarde grewit was, 435
With hys power in Scotland thocht to pafs,
For Erle Patrik had giffyn hym fic cunfaill.
Wallace gat wytt, and femblyt power haill,
Forty thoufand on Roflyn mur yar met.
Lords, he faid, yus is King Edwarde fet, 440
In contrar rycht to fek us in our land,
I hecht to God, and to yow, be my hand,
I fall hym meit, for all hys gret barnage,
Within Ingland, to fend our heretage;
Hys falfs defyr fall on hymfelff be feyn, 445
He fall us fynd in contrar off hys eyn;
Sen he with wrang has ryddyn yis regioun,
We fall pafs now in contrar off hys croun.
I will not bid gret lords with us fayr,
For myne entent I will playnly declar, 450
Our purpofs is oyir to wyn or de,
Quha zeildis hym, fall neuir ranfowmd be.
Ye barrons yan anfuerd hym worthely,
And faid, yai wald pafs with yair chewalry.
Hymfelf and Jop prowidyt yat menzhe, 455
Twenty thoufand off waillit men tuk he;
Harnes and horfs he gert amang yaim waill,
Wappynnys anew, yat mycht yaim weill awaill;
Grathyt yar men, yat cruell was and keyn,
Bettir in wer in warld coud nocht be feyn; 460

He baid ye laiff on laubour for to bide;
In gud aray fra Roflyn mur yai ryde.
At yair mufter gud Wallace couth yaim afs,
Quhat myfteryt ma in a power to pafs,
All off a will, as I trow fet ar we, 465
In playne battaill can nocht weill fcumfit be.
Our rewme is pur, waiftit be Sothroune blud,
Go wyn on yaim trefour, and oyir gud.
Ye oft inclynd all intill hummyll will,
And faid, yai fuld hys cummaundment fullfill. 470
Ye Erle Malcom with yir gud men is gayne,
Bot nayme off Rewill on hym he wald tak nayne.
Wallace hym knew a lord and full worthi,
At hys cunfaill he wrought full ftedfaftly;
Starkar he was, gyff yai fuld battaill feyn, 475
For he befor had in gud jornays beyn.
A man off ftrenth, yat has gud witt with all,
A haill regioune may confort at hys call.
As manly Ectour wrocht intill hys wer,
Agayne a hundreth cowntyt was hys fper; 480
Bot yat was nocht throuch hys ftrenth euirly,
Sic rewill he led off worthi chewalry.
Yir enfampillis war nobill for to ken.
Ectour I leiff, and fpek furth off our men.
Ye Knycht Cambell maid hym to yat wiage, 485
Off Lochow chieff yan was hys heretage.
Ye gud Ramfay furth to ye jornay went,
Schyr Jhon ye Grayme forthwart in hys entent,
Wallace cufyng, Adam, full worthi was,
And Robert Boid, full blythly furth yai pafs; 490

            Baithe

Baithe Awchinlek, and Richard off Lundy,
Lawdir and Hay, and Cetoun full worthy.
Yis ryoll oft, but reftyng, furth yai rid,
Till Browis feild, and yar a quhill yai bid.
Yan Wallace tuk with hym fyftye, but lefs,   495
Till Roxburgh zett raid fone, or he wald cefs.
Sothroune marwelld giff it fuld be Wallace,
Without Souerance come to perfew yat place.
Off Schyr Rauff Gray fome prefence couth he afs,
And wrand hym yus, forthwart he wald pafs,   500
Our purpofs is in Ingland for till ryde,
No tyme we haiff off fegyng now to byde,
Tak tent and her off our cummyng agayne,
Gyff our ye houfs fend me ye keyis in playn;
Yus I commaund befor yis witnes large,   505
Gyff zow will nocht, ramayne with all ye charge;
Bot yis be done, throuch force and I tak ze,
Out our ye wall yow fall be hyngyt hye.
With yat he turnd, and till hys oft can wend.
Yis ilk cummaund to Berweik fone he fend,   510
With gud Ramfay, yat was a worthi knycht.
Ye oft but mar, full awfully he dycht,
Began at Tweid, and fpard nocht at yai fand,
Bot brynt befor throuch all Northumyrland.
All Duram toune yai brynt up in a gleid,   515
Abbayis yai fpard, and kyrkis quhar yai zeid.
To Zork yai went, but baid, or yai wald blyn,
To byrn and fla off yaim he had na fyn.
Na fyn yai thocht ye famyn yai leitt us feill,
Bot Wilzham Wallace quyt our quarell weill.   520

            F 2.   Fortrace

Fortrace yai wan, and fmall caftellis keft doun,
With afpir wappynnys payit yair ranfoune.
Off prefonaris yai likit nocht to kep,
Quhom yai owrtuk, yai maid yair freynds to wepe,
Yai fawft na Sothroune for yair gret riches, 525
Off Sic koffre he cullit bot wrechitnes;
On to ye zetts and fabors off ye toune
Braithly yai brynt, and brak yair byggyngs doune,
At ye wallis affayed fyfeteyn dayis,
Till King Edwarde fend to yaim in yis wayis, 530
A knycht, a clerk, and a fquier off pefs,
And prayit hym fayr off byrnyng to cefs,
And hecht battaill, or fortye dayis war paft,
Souerance fo lang, gyff hym likit, till afs.
And als he fperd, quhy Wallace tuk on hand 535
Ye felloune ftryff, in defens off Scotland,
And faid, he merwelld on hys wit for thy,
Agayne Ingland was off fo gret party;
Sen ze haiff maid mekill off Scotland fre.
It war gret tyme for to lat malice be. 540
Wallace has herd ye meffage fay yair will,
With manly witt rycht yus he faid yaim till.
Ze may kna weill yat rycht yneuch we haiff,
Off hys Souerance I kep nocht for to craiff;
Becaufs I am a natyff Scotts man, 545
It is my dett to do all yat I can
To fend our kynryk out off dangyring.
Till hys defyr we will grant to fum thing,
Our oft fall cefs, for chans yat may betyd,
Yir fourtye dayis, bargane for till byd, 550
We

We fall do nocht, lefs yan it mowe in yow;
In hys refpyt myfelff couth neuir trew.
King Edwardis wrytt undir hys feill yai gaiff,
Be fourty dayis yat yai fuld battaill haiff.
Wallace yaim gaiff hys credence off yis thing.   555
Yair leyff yai tuk, fyne paffit to ye King,
And tauld hym haill how Wallace leit yaim feill,
Off your Soucrance he rekis nocht a deill;
Sic rewllyt men, fa awfull off affer,
Ar not cryftynyt, yan he ledis in wer.   560
Ye King anfuerd, and faid, it fuld be kend,
It cummys off witt enymyfs to commend;
Yai ar to dreid rycht gretly in certane,
Sadly yai think off armys yai haiff tane.
Leyff I yaim yus at cunfaill with ye King,   565
And off ye Scotts agayne to fpek fum thing.
Wallace trauountyt on ye fecund day,
Fra Zork yai paffit rycht in a gud aray;
North-weft yai paft in battaill bufkyt boun,
Yar Lugeyng tuk befyd Northallyrtoun,   570
And cryit hys pefs yair market for till ftand,
Yir fourtye dayis, for pepill off Ingland,
Quha yat lykit ony wittaill till fell.
Off all yair fer was mekill for to tell.
Schyr Rawff Rymut Captayne off Malcom was,   575
With gret power ordand be nycht to pafs
On Wallace oft, to mak fum jeperte.
Feyll Scotts men, yat duelt in yat cuntre,
Wyft off yis thing, and gaderyt to Wallace;
Yai maid hym wyfs off all yat futtell cace.   580

Gud Lundy yan till hym he callit yar,
And Hew ye Hay off Louthowort was ayr,
With thre thoufand yat worthely had wrocht,
Syne priwale out fra ye oft he focht.
Ye men he tuk, yat com till hym off new, 585
Gydys to be, for yai ye contre knew.
Ye oft he maid in gud quyet to be,
A fpace fra yaim he bufchyt prewale.
Schyr Rawff Rymut with fewyn thoufand com in,
On Wallace oft a jeperte to begyn. 590
Ye bufchement brak, or yai ye oft come ner,
On Southroune men ye worthi Scotts yai fter.
Thre thoufand haill was braithly brocht to ground,
Jornay yai focht, and fekyrly has found.
Schyr Rawff Rymut was ftekyt on a fper, 595
Thre thoufand flayne yat worthi war in wer.
Ye Sothroune wyft quhen yair Chyftane was dede,
To Maltoun faft yai fled, and left yat fted.
Wallace folowed with hys gud chewalry,
Amang Sothroune yai entryt fodeynly, 600
Inglis and Scotts into ye toune at anys.
Sothroune men fchot, and braithly keft doun ftanys,
Off yair awne rycht feyll yar haiff yai flayn.
Ye Scotts about, yat war off mekill mayn,
On grets ran, and ceffyt all ye tounc, 605
Derfly to dede ye Sothroune was dongyn doune.
Gud Wallace yar has found full gud ryches,
Jowellis and gold, baith wappynnys and harnes,
Spoulzeid ye toun off wyn, and off wittaill,
All off fend with caryagis off gret waill. 610

Thre

Thre dayis ſtill within ye toune yai baid,
Syne brak doun werk yat worthely was maid.
Wyffs and childir yai put out off ye toune,
Na man he fawſt yat was off yat natioune.
Quhen Scotts had tayne to turfs at yair defyr, 615
Wallis yai brak, fyne ſet ye laiff in fyr.
Ye temir werk yat brynt up all in playn,
On ye ferd day till hys oſt raid agayne,
Gert caſt a dyk yat mycht ſum ſtrynthyng be,
To kepe ye oſt fra ſodeyn jeperte. 620
Yan Ingliſmen was rycht gretly agaſt,
Fra north and ſouth ontill yair King yai paſt,
At Pomfray lay, and held a parlement.
To gyff battaills ye lordis couth nocht conſent,
Leſs Wallace war off Scotland crownyt King; 625
Yar confaill fand it war a peralous thing;
For yocht yai wan, yai wan bot as yai war,
And gyff yai tynt, yai loſſyt Ingland for cuirmair,
A payn war, put in to ye Scotts hand.
And yis Decret yar witt amang yaim fand, 630
Gyff Wallace wald apon hym tak ye croun,
To gyff battaill yai ſuld be redy boun.
Ye ſamyn meſſage till hym yai ſend agayn,
And yair entent yai tald hym into playn.
Wallace yaim chargyt hys preſens till abſent, 635
Hys cunſaill callyt, and ſchawit yaim hys entent,
He and hys men deſyryt battaill till haiff,
Be ony wayis, off Ingland our ye laiff.
He ſaid, fyrſt, it war a our hie thing,
Agayne ye faith to reyff my rychtwis King, 640

I am

I am hys man, born natiff off Scotland,
To wer ye croun I will nocht tak on hand;
To fend ye rewm it is my dett be fkill,
Lat God abowe reward me as he will.
Sum bad Wallace apon hym tak ye croun.   645
Wyfs men faid, nay, it war bot deryfioun,
To croun hym King bot woice off ye parlyment,
For yai wyft nocht gyff Scotland wald confent.
Oyir fum faid, it was ye wrangwis place.
Yus demyt yai on mony diuerfs cace.   650
Yis Knycht Cambell, off witt a worthi man,
As I faid ayr, was prefent with yaim yan,
Herd and anfuerd, quhen mony faid yair will,
Yis war ye beft, wald Wallace grant yartill,
To croun hym King folemly for a day,   655
To get ane end off all our lang delay.
Ye gud Erle Malcom faid yat Wallace mycht,
As for a day, in fens off Scotlands rycht,
Refawe ye croun, as in a fer off wer,
Ye pepill all till hym gaiff yair confent;   660
Malcom off auld was lord off ye parlyment.
Zeit wallace tholyt, and leit yaim fay yair will,
Quhen yai had demyt be mony diuerfs fkill,
In hys awn mynd he abhorryt with yis thing.
Ye commouns cryit, mak Wallace crownyt King.   665
Yan fmylyt he, and faid it fuld nocht be,
As termys fchort, ze get na mar for me;
Undyr colour we mon our anfuer mak,
Bot fic a thing I will nocht on me tak;
I fuffer zow to fay yat it is fa,   670

It

It war a fcorn ye croun on me to ta.
Yai wald nocht lat ye meffage off Ingland
Cum yaim amang, or yai fuld undirftand.
Twa knychts paffit to ye meffage agayne,
Maid yaim to trow Wallace was crownyt in playne,
Gart yaim traift weill yat yis was futh faft thing.
Delyuyryt yus yai paffit to yair King,
To Pomfrait went, and tald yat yai had feyn
Wallace crownyt, quharoff ye lordis was teyn,
In Barrate wox, in parlyment quhar yai ftud.   680
Yan faid yai all, yir tithands ar nocht gud,
He did fa weyll into yair tymys befor,
And now yair King, he will do mekill mor.
A fortunyt man, nothing gois hym agayne,
To gyff battaill we fall it rew a payne.   685
Ane oyir faid, and battaill will he haiff,
Or ftroy our land, na trefour may us faiff;
In hys conqueft, fen fyrft he couth begyn,
He fellis nocht bot takis quhat he may wyn;
For Inglifmen he fetts no doym but ded,   690
Pryce off pennyis may mak us na ramed.
Ane Wodeftok faid, ze werk nocht as ye wyfs,
Gyff at ze tak ye awentur off fupprice;
For thoch we wyn yat ar intill Ingland,
Ye laiff ar ftark agaynys us for to ftand;   695
Be Wallace faiff, oyir yai count bot fmall;
For yat methink yis war ye beft off all,
To kepe our ftrenth of caftell and off walltown,
Swa fall we fend ye fek off yis regioun;
Thouch north be brynt, bettir off fufferans be,   700

Yan

Yan fet all Ingland on a jeperte.
Yai grantyt all, as Wodftok can yaim fay,
And yus yai put ye battaill on delay,
And keft yaim haill for oyir gouernance,
Agayn Wallace to wyrk fum ordinance. 705
Yus Wallace has in playn difcumfit haill,
Agayn King Edwarde all hys ftrang battaill;
For throuch falfheid, and yar fubtelite,
Yai thocht he fuld, for gret neceffite,
And faute off fude, to fteyll out off ye land; 710
And yis Decret yair witt amang yaim fand.
Yai gert ye King cry all yair merket doun,
Fra Trent to Tweid off thro fayr and fre toun,
Yat in yai boundis na man fuld wittaill leid,
Sic ftuff, nor wyn, on na lefs payn bot deid; 715
Yis ilk Decret yai gaiff in yair parlyment.
Off Scotts forfuth to fpek is myn entent.
Wallace lay ftill, quhill fourty dayis was gayn,
And fyffe atour, bot perance faw he nayn
Battaill till haiff, as yair promyfs was maid; 720
He gert difplay agayne hys Baner braid,
Rapreiffyt Edwarde rycht gretlye off yis thing,
Bawchyllyt hys feyll, blew out on yat fals King,
As a tyrand turnd bak and tuk hys gait.
Yan Wallace maid full mony byggyng hayt; 725
Yai raffyt fyr, brynt up Northallartoun,
Agayne throuch Zork-fchyre bauldly maid yaim boun,
Dyftroyed ye land, as fer as euir yai ryde,
Sewyn myle about yai brynt on ayir fyde;
Palyce yai fpylt, gret towris can cunfound, 730
Wrocht

Wrocht ye Sothroune mony werkand wound.
Wedowis wepyt with forow in yair fang,
Madennys murnyt with gret wenyng amang.
Yai fparyt nocht bot wemen and ye kirk.
Yir worthi Scotts off laubour wald nocht yrk. 735
Abbayis gaiff yaim rycht largly to yair fud,
Till all kyrk man yai did nothing bot gud.
Ye temperall land yai fpoulzeit at yair will,
Gud gardens gay, and Orcharts gret yai fpill.
Till Zork yai went yir wermen off renoune, 740
A fege yai fet rycht fadly to ye toune.
For gret defens yai garneft yaim within.
A felloune falt without yai can begyn;
Gert woid ye oft in four parts about,
With wachys feyll, yat no man fuld ufche out. 745
Abowne ye toune, apon ye fouth part fid,
Yar Wallace wald and gud Lundy abid.
Erle Malcom fyne at ye weft zett abaid,
With hym ye Boid yat gud jornays had maid.
Ye Knycht Cambell, off Lochow was lord, 750
At ye north zett, and Ramfay maid yaim ford.
Schyr Jhon ye Grayme, yat worthi was in wer,
Awchinlek, Crawfurd, with full manlik affer,
At ye eft part bauldly yai boune to byd.
A thoufand archars apon ye Scotts fyd 755
Diffcuyryt yaim amang ye four party.
Fyfe thoufand bowmen in ye tour for yi,
Within ye wallis arayit yaim full rycht,
Twelfe thoufand and ma yat fembly was to fycht.
Yan faid Wallace, yar zond apon a playn, 760

In feild to fecht methink we fuld bewayn.
Yan failzeit yai rycht faft on ilka fyd.
Ye worthi Scotts, yat bauldly durft abyd,
With fper and fcheild, for gounnys had yai nayne,
Within ye dykys yai gert feill Sothroune grayn; 765
Arowis yai fchot als fers as ony fyr,
Attour ye wall, yat flawmyt in gret ire
Throuch byrneis brycht, with hedys fyn off fteyll,
Ye Sothroune blud yai leit na freindfchip feyll,
Our fchefferand harnes fchot ye blud fo fcheyn. 770
Ye Inglis men, yat cruell was and keyn,
Kepyt yar toune, and fendyt yar full faft,
Fagaldys off fyr amang ye oft yai caft,
Up pyk and ter on feyll fowys yai lent,
Mony war hurt or yai fra wallis went. 775
Stanys and fpryngaldis yai caft out fo faft,
And gadys of irne, maid mony groym agaft:
Bot, neuiryeles, ye Scotts yat was without,
Ye toune full oft yai fet into gret dout,
Yair bulwerk brynt rycht brymly off ye toun, 780
Yair barmkyn wan, and gret garrets keft doun.
Yus failzeit yai, on ilk fyd, with gret mycht.
Ye day was gayn, and cummyn was ye nycht.
Ye wery oft yan drew yaim fra ye toun,
Set out wachis, for reftyng maid yaim boun; 785
Wyfche woundis with wyn off yaim yat was unfound,
For nayn was dede in gret myrth yai abound.
Feill men was hurt, but na murnyng yai maid,
Confyrmyt ye fege, and ftedfaftly abaid,
Quben yat ye fon on morow raifs up rycht, 790

Befor

Befor ye Chyftanys femblit yai full rycht,
And mendis thoucht of ye toune yai fuld tak,
For all ye fens yat ye Sothroune mycht mak;
Arayit agayne, as yai began befor,
About ye toune yai failze wondyr for, 795
With felfoune fchot atour ye wall fo fcheyn,
Feill Inglifmen, yat cruell was and keyn,
With fchot was flayn, for all yair targs ftrang,
Byrftyt helmys, mony to erd yai dang;
Brycht byrnand fyr yai keft till euir ilk zet, 800
Ye entrefs yus in perall oft yai fet.
Ye Defendours was off fo fell defens,
Kepyt yair toune with ftrenth and excellens.
And yus ye day yai dryff on, to ye nycht
To palzounns bownyt mony wery wycht. 805
All yrk off wer, ye toune was ftrang to wyn,
Off artailre, and nobill men with gyn.
Quhen yat yai trowyt ye Scotts was all at reft,
For jeperte ye Inglifmen yaim keft.
Schyr Jhon Nourtoun was knawyn worthi and wycht,
Schyr Wilzham off Leis, graithit yaim yat nycht,
With fyffe thoufand weyll garnyft and fawage,
Apon ye Scotts yai thocht to mak fcrymmage,
And at a zet ufchyt out haiftely
On Erle Malcom, and hys gud chewalry. 815
To chak ye wache Wallace and ten had beyn,
Rydand about, and has yair cummyng feyn.
He gert ane blaw was in hys cumpany,
Ye redy men arayit yaim haiftely.
Feill off ye Scotts ilk nycht in harnes baid, 820

Be ordinance, for yai fic rewill had maid;
With fchort awyfs togyddyr ar yai went,
Apon yair fais, quhar feill Sothroune was fchent.
Wallace knew wéyll ye Erle to haifty was,
For yi he fped hym to ye prefs to pafs; 825
A fuerd off wer intill hys hand he bar,
Ye fyrft he hyt ye crag in fondyr fchar;
Ane oyir awkwart apon ye face tuk he,
Wyfar and frount bathe in ye feild gert fle.
Ye hardy Erle befor hys men furth paft, 830
Into ye prefs, quhar feill war fechtand faft;
A fcherand fuerd bar drawyn in hys hand,
Ye fyrft was fey yat he befor hym fand.
Quhen Wallace and he war togyddir fet
Yar leftyt nane agayn yaim yat yai met, 835
Bot ayir dede, or ellis fled yaim fray.
Be yis ye oft all in gud aray
With ye gret fcry affemblit yaim about;
Yan ftud ye Sothroune in a felloune dout.
Wallace knew weill ye Inglifmen wald fle, 840
For yi he preyft in ye thikkeft to be,
Hewand full faft on quhat fege yat he focht,
Agaynys hys dynt fyn fteyll awailzeit nocht.
Wallace off hand, fen Arthour, had na mak,
Quhom he hyt rycht was ay dede off a ftrak, 845
Yat was weill knawin in mony place, and yar
Quhom Wallace hyt he deryt ye Scotts no mar.
Als all hys men did cruelly and weyll,
At come to ftrak, yat mycht ye Sothroune feyll.
Ye Inglis men fled, and left ye feild playnly. 850
Ye

Ye worthi Scotts wroucht fa hardely,
Schyr Jhon off Nourton in yat place was dede,
And twelfe hundreth, withoutyn ony ramede.
Yar mony was left into ye feild and flayn,
Ye laiff raturnyt into ye toune agayn, 855
And ruyt full far yat euyr yai furth coud found,
Amang yaim was full mony werkand wound.
Ye oft agayne ilk ane to yair ward raid,
Cummandyt wachis, and na mayr noyis maid,
Bot reftyt ftill quhill yat ye brycht day dew. 860
Agayne began ye toune to failze new.
All yus yai wrocht with full gud worthines,
Affailzeit far with wytt and hardynes.
Ye ofts wittaill worth fcant, and failzeit faft,
Yus lay yai yar, quhill diuerfs dayis war paft, 865
Ye land waiftyt, and meit was fer far to wyn;
Bot yat wyft nocht ye ftuff yat was within,
Yai dred full far for yair awn waryfoun.
For Souerance prayit ye power off ye toune;
To fpek with Wallace yai defyryt faft, 870
And he aperyt, and fperyt quhat yai aft.
Ye Mayr anfuerd, faid, we wald gyff ranfoun,
To pafs zour way, and der no mayr ye toune;
Gret fchaym it war yat we fuld zolden be,
And townys haldyn off lefs power yan we; 875
Ze may nocht wyn us futhly yocht ze byde,
We fall giff gold, and ze wald fra us ryde;
We may gyff battaill, durft we for our King,
Sen he has left it, war ane our hie thing
Till us to de, without hys ordinance, 880

Yis toune off hym we hald in gouernance.
Wallace anfuerd, off zour gold rek we nocht,
It is for battaill yat we hydder focht;
We had leiffer haiff battaill off Ingland,
Yan all ye gold yat gud King Arthour fand   885
On ye mont Mychell, quhar he ye gyantt flew;
Gold may be gayn, bot worfchip is ay new.
Zour King promyft yat we fuld battaill haiff,
Hys wrytt yarto undyr hys feyll he gaiff;
Lettir nor band, ye fe, may nocht awaill,   890
Befor yis toun he hecht to gyff battaill;
Me think we fuld on hys men wengyt be,
Apon our kyn mony gret wrang wrocht he,
Hys dewyl lik deid he did into Scotland.
Ye Mayr faid, fchyr, rycht yus we undirftand,   895
We haiff na charge quhat our King gers us do;
Bot in yis kynd we fall be bundyn zow to,
Sum part of gold to gyff you with gud will,
And nocht efftyr to wait yow with na ill,
Be na kyn meyn, ye power off yis toun,   900
Bot gyff our King mak hym to battaill boun.
Into ye oft was mony worthi man,
With Wallace, ma yan I now rekyn can.
Bettir it was, for at hys will yai wrocht,
Yocht he was beft, no oyir lak we nocht,   905
All feruit thank to Scotland euirmair,
For manheid witt ye quhilk yai fchawit yair.
Ye haill cunfaill yus demyt yaim amang,
Ye toune to fege yaim thocht it was to lang,
And nocht a payn to wyn it be no flycht.   910

Ye

Ye cunfaill fand it was ye beft yai mycht,
Sum gold to tak, gyff yat yai get no mar,
Syne furth yair way in yair wiage yai far.
Yan Wallace faid, myfelf will nocht confent,
Bot gyff yis toune mak us yus playne content, 915
Tak our Baner, and fet it on ye wall,
For yair power our rewme has ridyn all,
Zoldyn to be, quhen we lik yaim to tak,
Intill Ingland refidens gyff we mak.
Yis anfuer fone yai fend into ye Mayr. 920
Yan yai confent, ye remayn yat was yar,
Ye Baner tuk, and fet it on ye toune,
Till Scotland was hys honour and renounc.
Yat Baner yar was fra aucht hours to none,
Yair finance maid delyueryt gold full fone, 925
Fyftye thoufand pund all gud gold off Ingland,
Ye oft refawyt, with wittaill haboundand;
Bathe breid and wyne rycht glaidly furth yai gaiff;
And oyir ftuff at yai likit to haiff.
Twentye dayis out ye oft ramaynit yar, 930
Bot want off wittaill gert yaim fra it far;
Zeit ftill off pefs ye oft lugyt all nycht,
Quhill on ye morn ye fone was ryffyn on hycht,
In Aprill amang ye fchawis fcheyn,
Quhen ye paithment was clad in tendyr greyn; 935
Plefand war it till ony creatur,
In lufty lyff yat tym for till endur.
Yir gud wer men had fredome largly,
Bot fude was fcant, yai mycht get nayn to by.
Turfyt tents, and in ye contre raid, 940

On Inglifmen full gret herfchipe yai maid;
Brynt and brak doun byggyns, fparyt yai nocht,
Rycht worthi wallis full law to ground yai brocht.
All mydlen land yai brynt up in a fyr,
Brak parkis doune deftroyit all ye fchyr; 945
Woyld der yai flew for oyir befts was nayn,
Yir wermen tuk off venyfoune gud wayn.
Towart ye fouth yai turnyt at ye laft,
Maid byggyngs bar als fer as euir yai paft.
Ye commouns all to London ar yai went, 950
Befor ye King, and tald hym yar entent,
And faid, yai fuld, but he gert Wallace cefs,
Forfaik yair faith, and tak yaim till hys pefs.
Na herrald yar durft yan to Wallace pafs,
Quharoff ye king gretly agrewit was. 955
Yus Edwarde left his pepill into baill,
Contrar Wallace he wald nocht gyff battaill.
Nor byd in feild for nocht yat yai couth fay,
Gaiff our ye caufs, to London paft hys way.
At men off wit yis queftioune her I afs, 960
Amang noblis gyff euyr ony yat was,
Sa lang throw force in Ingland lay on cafs,
Synce Brudus deit but battaill bot Wallace.
Gret Julius ye empyr had in hand,
Twyfs off force he was put off Ingland. 965
Wycht Arthour als off wer quhen yat he prewit,
Twyfs yai faucht, fuppofs yai war myfchewyt.
Awfull Edwarde durft nocht Wallace abid,
In playn battaill for all Ingland fo wid,
In London he lay, and tuk hym to hys reft, 970
And

And brak hys wow, quhilk hald yow for ye beſt;
Rycht clayr it is to ranſek yis queſtioun,
Deyme as ze leſt, gud men off diſcretioun.
To my ſentence breyſſly will I paſs,
Quhen Wallace yus throw Zork-ſchyre jowrnat was,
Wittaill as yan was nayne left in ye land,
Bot in houſſis quhar it mycht be warrand.
Ye oſt hereoff abaiſyt was to byd;
Fra fude ſcantyt na pleſance was yat tyd;
Sum baid ryd hayme, ſum baid ryd forthirmar, 980
Wallace callyt Jop, and ſaid to hym rycht yar,
Yow knawis ye land, quhar maiſt abaundance is,
Be yow our gyd, and yan we ſall nocht myſs
Wittaill to fynd, yat wait I wondir weyll,
Yow has, I traiſt, off Ingland mekill feyll. 985
Ye King and he to ſtark ſtrenthis ar gayn,
Bot jeperte, now perill haiff we nayn.
Yan Jop ſaid, be ze gydyt be me,
Ye bowndandeſt part off Ingland ze ſall ſe;
Off wyn and quheyt yar is in Rychmount-ſchyr, 990
And oyir ſtuff off fud yat ye deſyr,
Quharoff I trow ze ſall be weyll content.
Ye oſt was glaid and yidderwart yai went.
Mony trew Scotts war ſemblyt in yat land,
To Wallace come weyll ma yan nyne thouſand; 995
Off priſone part, ſum had in lawbour wrocht,
Fra ayir parts full faſt till hym yai ſocht.
Wallace was blyth off our awn natyff kyn
Yat come till hym, off baill yat yai war in;
And all ye oſt off comfort was ye blythar, 1000

Fra

Fra yair awn folk was multipliand ye mar.
In Richmunt-fchyr yai fand a gret bundance,
Breid, ayll and wyn, with oyir purueance;
Brak parkis doun, and flew beftis mony ane,
Off wyld and tayme, forfuth yai fparyt nane. 1005
Throuchout ye land yai paft in gud aray;
A fembly place fa fand yai in yar way,
Quhilk Ramfwaith hecht, as Jop hymfelf yai tald;
Fehew was Lord and Captayne in yat hald.
A hundreth men was femblyt in yat place; 1010
To fawe yaimfelf and yar gud fra Wallace;
A ryoll fted, faft by a foreft fyd,
With turretts fayr, and garretts off gret pryd,
Beildyt about, rycht likly to be wycht,
Awfull it was till ony mannis fycht; 1015
Feill men aboune on ye wallis bufkyt beyn,
In gud armour, yat burnyft was full fcheyn.
Ye oft paft by, and bot wefyt yat place;
Zen yai within on lowd defyt Wallace,
And trumpatts blew with mony werlik foun. 1020
Yan Wallace faid, had we zon gallands doun,
On ye playn ground, yai wald mor fobyr be.
Yan Jop faid, fchyr, yow gart hys brodyr de,
In harrold weid, ye wait, on Tynto-hill.
Wallace anfuerd, fo wald I with gud will, 1125
Had I hymfelff, bot we may nocht yaim der,
Gud men mon thoill off harlotts fcorn in wer.
Schyr Jhon ye Grayme wald at a bykkyr beyn:
Bot Wallace fone yat gret perell has feyn,
Commaundyt hym to lett hys feruice be, 1030

We

We haiff na men to waift in fic degre;
Wald ye yaim harm, I knaw ane oyir gait,
Quhow we throuch fyr within fall mak yaim hait;
Fyr has beyn ay full felloune into wer,
On fic a place it ma do mekill der; 1135
Yair auld bulwerk I fe off wyddryt ayk,
War it in fyr, yai mycht not byd a ftraik,
Houffis and wode is her eneuch plente,
Quha hewis beft off yis forreft lat fe;
Pull houffis doun, we fall not want a deill, 1040
Ye auld temyr will ger ye greyn byrn weill.
At hys cummaund full befyly yai wrocht,
Gret wode in haift about ye houfs yai brocht.
Ye bulwerk wan yair men off armys brycht,
To ye barmkyn laid temyr apon hycht. 1045
Yan bowmen fchot to kep yaim fra ye caft;
Ye wall about had feftnyt fyris faft.
Women and barnys on Wallace faft yai cry,
On kneis yai fell, and afkyt hym mercy.
At a quartar, quhar fyr had nocht ourtayn, 1050
Yai tuk yaim out fra caftell off ftayn,
Syne let ye fyr with brundys brym and bauld,
Ye rude low raifs full heich aboune yat hauld.
Barrellis off pyk for ye defens was hungyn yar,
All ftrak in fyr, ge myfcheiff was ye mar. 1055
Quhen ye brym fyr attour ye place was paft,
Yan yai within mycht noyir fchut no caft.
Als beftiall, as horfs and nowt, within,
Amang ye fyr yai maid a hidwyfs din.
Ye armyt men in harnes was fo hait, 1060

Sum

Sum doun to ground dufchit but mar debait;
Sum lap, fum fell into ye felloune fyr,
Smoryt to dede, and brynt bath bayn and lyr,
Ye fyr brak in at all opynnys about,
Nayn baid on loft, fo felloune was ye dout. 1065
Fehew hymfelff lap rudly fra ye hycht,
Throuch all ye fyr can on ye barmkyn lyckt.
With a gud fuerd Wallace ftrak off hys hed,
Jop hynt it up, and turft fra yat fted.
Fyffe hundreth men, yat war into yat place, 1070
Gat nayne away, bot dede withoutyn grace.
Wallace baid ftill with hys power yat nycht;
Apon ye morn ye fyr had failzeit mycht.
Befor ye zett, quhar it was brynt on breid,
A red yai maid, and to ye Caftell zeid, 1075
Strak doun ye zett, and tuk yat yai mycht wyn,
Jewllis and gold, gret riches was yarin;
Spulzeit ye place, and left nocht ellis yar,
Bot beftis, brynt bodyis, and wallis bar.
Yan tuk yai hyr, yat wyff was to Fehew, 1080
Gaiff yis cummand, as fche was women trew,
To turfs yat hed to London to King Edwarde.
Sche it refawit with gret forow on hart.
Wallace hymfelff yar chargis till hyr gaiff,
Say to zour King, bot gyff I battaill haiff, 1085
At London zetts we fall affalzie fayr,
In yis moneth we think for to be yar;
Trafts in treuth, will God, we fall nocht faill,
Bot I rafyft throw charge off our cunfaill;
Ye fouthmaift part off Ingland we fall fe, 1090
Bot

Bot he fek pefs, or ellis bargan with me;
Apon a tyme he chargy me on yis wyfs,
Rycht bouftoufly to mak till hym feruice;
Sic fall he haiff, as he us caufs had maid.
Yan mowit yai without langar abaid. 1095
Delyueryt fche was fra yis gud chewalry,
Towart London fche focht rycht ernyftfully;
On to ye tour, but mar procefs fche went,
Quhar Edwarde lay fayr murnyng in hys entent.
Hys newois hede, quhen he faw it was brocht, 1100
Sa gret forow fadly apon hym focht,
With gret unefs apon hys feit he ftud,
Wepand for wo for hys der tendyr blud.
Ye cunfaill raifs, and prayit hym for to cefs,
We lofs Ingland bot gyff ye purchefs pefs. 1105
Yan Wodftok faid, yis is my beft cunfaill,
Tak pefs a tyme as for our awn awaill,
Or we tyne mar flaik off our curage,
Treft ze may get help to your barnage.
Ye King grantyt, and baid yaim meffage fend; 1110
Na man was yar yat durft to Wallace wend.
Ye Queyn apperyt, and faw yis gret diftance,
Weill born fche was off ye rycht blud off France,
Sche trowit weill yarfor to fped ye mar,
Hyrfelff purpoft in yat meffage to far. 1115
Als fche forthocht yat ye King tuk on hand,
Agayne ye rycht fo oft to reyff Scotland.
And feill faid, ye wengeance hapnyt yar,
Off gret murthyr hys men maid intill Ayr.
Yus demyt yai ye cunfaill yaim amang. 1120

To

To yis effett ye Queyn bownyt to gang;
Quhen fche has feyn ilk man forfak yis thing,
On kneis fche fell, and afkyt at ye King,
Sowerane, fche faid, gyff it zour willis be,
At I defyr yon Chuftane for to fe,   1125
For he is knawin baith hardy, wyfs, and trew,
Perchance he will erar on wemen rew,
Yan on zour men; zow haiff don hym fic der,
Quhen he yaim feis, it mowis hym ay to wer.
To help yis land I wald mak my trawaill,   1130
It ma nocht fcaith, fuppofs it do na waill.
Ye lordis all off hyr defyr was fayn,
On to ye King yai maid inftans in playn,
Yat fche mycht pafs. Ye King, with awkwart will,
Halff into ire, has confent yartill.   1135
Sum off yaim faid, ye Queyn luffyt Wallace,
For ye gret woice off hys hie nobilnes.
A hardy man, yat is likly with all,
Gret fawour will off fortoun till hym fall,
Anent wemen is feyne in mony place,   1140
So hapnyt it in hys tyme with Wallace.
In hys ryffyng he was a luffar trew,
And chefyt ane, quhilk Inglifmen hyr flew.
Zeit I fay nocht ye Queyn wald on hyr tak,
All for hys luff, fic trawaill for to mak.   1145
Sche graithit hyr apon a gudlye wifs,
With gold and ger and folk at hyr dewifs;
Ladyis with hyr, nane oyir wald yai fend,
And ald preyfts, yat weill ye cuntre kend.
Lat I ye Queyn to meffage redy dycht,   1150
                                          And

And fpek furth mar off Wallace trawaill rycht.
Ye worthi Scotts amang yair enymyfs raid,
Full gret deftructioune amang ye Sothroune yai maid,
Waiftit about ye land on ayir fyd,
Na wer men yan durft in yair way abyd; 1155
Yai ranfoun nane, bot to ye dede yai dycht,
In mony fteid maid fyrs braid and brycht.
Ye oft was blyth, and in a gud eftate,
Na power was at wald mak yaim debaite;
Gret ryches wan off gold and gud yaim till, 1160
Leyffyng enewch to tak at yair awn will.
In awfull fer yai trawaill throuch ye land,
Maid byggyngs bar yat yai befor yaim fand;
Gret barmkynnys brak off fleds ftark and ftrang;
Yar wycht wer men off trawaill thocht nocht lang. 1165
South in ye land rycht erneftfully yai focht,
To Santt Allbawnys bot harm yar did yai nocht;
Ye power fend yaim wyn and wenyfoun,
Refrefchyt ye oft with gud in gret fufioun.
Ye nycht apperyt quhen yai war at ye place, 1170
Yan herbreyt yaim fra ynce a litill fpace,
Chefyt a fted quhar yai fuld byd all nycht,
Tents on ground, and palzonis proudly pycht;
Into a waill, be a fmall rywer fayr,
On ayir fid yuhar wyld der maid repayr; 1175
Set wachis out, yat wyfly couth yaim kepe,
To fouppar went, and tymfly yai flepe;
Off meit and fleip yai cefs with fuffifiance.
Ye nycht was myrk, our drayff ye dyrkfull chance.
Ye mery day fprang fra ye oryent, 1180

With bemys brycht enlumynyt ye occident.
After Titan, Phebus upryfyt fayr,
Heich in ye fper, ye fignes maid declayr.
Zephers began hys morow courfs,
Ye fwete wapour yus fra ye ground refourfs;   1185
Ye humyll breyth doun fra ye Hewen awaill,
In euery meide, bathe fyrth, forreft and daill.
Ye cler rede amang ye rochis rang,
Throuch greyn branchis quhar byrds blythly fang,
With joyus wois in hewynly armony.   1190
Yan Wallace thocht it was no tyme to ly;
He croyffit hym, fyne fodeynle up raifs,
To tak ye ayr out off hys palzon gaes.
Maifter Jhon Blar was redy to rawefs,
In gud entent fyne bownyt to ye mefs.   1195
Quhen it was don, Wallace can hym aray,
In hys armour, quhilk gudly was and gay.
Hys fchenand fchoys, yat burnyft was full beyne,
Hys leg harnes he clappyt on fa clene,
Pullane greis he braiffit on full faft,   1200
A clofs byrny, with mony fekyr clafp,
Breyft plait, brazars, yat worthi was in wer;
Befid hym furth Jop couth hys bafnet ber;
Hys glytterand glowis grawin on ayir fyd,
He femyt weill in battaill till abyde;   1205
Hys gud gyrdill, and fyne hys burly brand,
A ftaff off fteyll he gryppyt in hys hand.
Ye oft hym blyft, and prayit God, off hys Grace,
Hym to conway fra all myftymyt cace.
Adam Wallace and Boid furth with hym zeid,   1210
Be

Be a rywer throuchout a forryſt meid;
And as yai walk atour ye feylds fa greyn,
Out off ye fouth yai faw quhar at ye Queyn,
Towart ye oſt come ridand fobyrly,
And fyfty ladyis was in hyr cumpany,   1215
Waillyt off wyt, and demyt off renoun,
Sum wedowis war, and fum off religioun;
And fewyn preyſts yat entrit war in age;
Wallace to ſic did neuir gret owtrage,
Bot gyff till hym yai maid a gret offens.   1220
Yus prochyt yai on towart yair prefens.
At ye palzoun, quhar yai ye lyown faw,
To grounde yai lycht, and fyne on kneis can faw,
Prayan'd for pefs, yai cry with petous cher.
Erle Malcom faid, our Chyftane is not her;   1225
He bad hyr ryfs, and faid it was nocht rycht,
A Queyn on kneis till ony lawar wycht.
Up by ye hand ye gud Erle has hyr tayn,
Atour ye bent to Wallace ar yai gayn.
Quhen fche hym faw, fche wald haiff knelyt doune;
In armys fone he caucht yis Queyn with croun,
And kyffyt hyr withoutyn wordis mor,
Sa dyd he neuir to na Sothroune befor.
Madeym, he faid, rycht welcum mot ze be,
Quhow pleffis zow our oſtyng for to fe.   1235
Rycht weill, fche faid, off freindfchipe haiff we neid,
God grant ze wald off our nefs to fpeid.
Suffyr we mon, fuppofs it lik us ill,
Bot trafts, weill it is contrar our will;
Ze fall ramayn, with yis lord I mon gang,   1240

Fra zour prefens we fall nocht tary lang.
Ye Erle and he on to ye palzeon zeid,
With gud awifs to deym mar off yis deid.
Till cunfaill fone Wallace gert call yaim to,
Lordis he faid, ze wait quhat is ado, 1245
Off yair cummyng myfelff has na plefance,
Herfor mon we wyrk with ordinance;
Wemen may be com tempnying into wer,
Amang fullis yat can yaim nocht forber.
I fay nocht yis be yir, nor zeit ze Queyn, 1250
I trow it be bot gud yat fche will meyn;
Bot fampyll tak off lang tyme paft by;
At Rownfywaill ye trefoun was playnly
Be wemen maid, yat Ganzelon with hym brocht,
And Turke wyn forber yaim couth yai nocht: 1255
Lang ufs in wer gert yaim defyr yair will,
Quhilk brocht Charlis to felloune lofs and ill;
Ye flour off France, withoutyn redemptioun,
Throuch yat foull dede, was brocht to confufioune.
Commaund zour men yarfor in priway wyfs, 1260
On payn off lyff yai wyrk nocht on fic wyfs;
Nane fpek with yaim, bot wyfsmen off gret waill,
At lords ar, and fuorn to yis cunfaill.
Yis charge yai did als wyfly as yai mycht,
Yis ordynance throw all ye oft was wrocht. 1265
He and ye Erle bathe to ye Queyn yai went,
Refawyt hyr fayr, and brocht hyr till a tent,
To dyner bownyt als gudly as yai can,
And ferwit was with mony likly man.
Gud purwiance ye Queyn had with hyr wrocht, 1270

A fey

A fey fche tuk off all thing yat yai brocht.
Wallace perfawyt, and faid, we haiff na dreid,
I can nocht trow ladyis wald do fic deid,
To poyfoun men, for all Ingland to wyn.
Ye Queyn anfuerd, gyff poyfoun be yarin, 1275
Off ony thing quhilk is brocht her with me,
Apon myfelff fyrft forow fall ze fe.
Sone eftir meit a Marchell gart abfent,
Bot lordis, and yai yat fuld to cunfaill went.
Ladyis apperyt in prefens with ye Queyn. 1280
Wallace afkyt quhat hyr cummyng mycht meyn.
For pefs, fche faid, at we haiff to yow focht,
Yis byrnand wer in baill has mony brocht;
Ze grant us pefs, for hym yat deit on tre.
Wallace anfuerd, madeym yat may nocht be, 1285
Ingland has doyne fa gret harmys till us,
We may nocht pafs, and lychtly leiffit yus.
Zeifs faid ye Queyne, for cryftyn folk we ar,
For Godds faik, fen we defyr na mar,
We awcht pefs. Madeym, yat I deny, 1290
Ye perfyt caufs I fall zone fchaw for quhy;
Ze feke na pefs, bot for your awne awaill:
Quhen your fals King had Scotland gryppyt haill,
For na kyn thing yat he befor hym fand,
He wald nocht thoill ye rycht blud in our land, 1295
Bot reft yar rent, fyne put yaimfelff to ded,
Ranfoun off gold mycht mak us na remed;
Hys fell fals wer fall on hymfelff be feyn.
Yan fobyrly till hym anfuerd ye Queyn,
Off yir wrangs amends war moft fair. 1300

H 3   Madeym,

Madeym, he faid, off hym we ask na mar,
Bot at he wald byd us into Battaill,
And God be juge, he kennys ye mattir haill.
Sic mendis, fche faid, war not rycht gud think me;
Pefs now war beft, and it mycht purcheft be: 1305
Wald ze grant pefs, and trwyfs with us tak,
Throuch all Ingland we fuld gar prayers mak
For yow, and yaim at in ye wer war loft.
Yan Wallace faid, quhar fic thing cummys throuch boft,
Prayer off fors, quhar fo at it be wrocht, 1310
Till us helpis litill, or ellis nocht.
Warly fche faid, yus wyffmen has us kend,
Ay eftir wer pefs is ye finall end;
Quharfor ze fuld off your gret malice cefs,
Ye end off wer is cherete and pefs. 1315
Pefs is in Hewyn, with blyfs and leftandnas,
We fall befeke ye Pepe, off hys hie grace,
Till cummaund, pefs fen we may do na mar.
Madeym, he faid, or your purchefs cum yar,
Mendys we think off Ingland for to haiff. 1320
Quhat fet yow yus, fche faid, for God zow faiff,
Fra violent wer at ye lik nocht to duell.
Madeym, he faid, ye futh I fall yow tell.
Eftir ye dayt off Alexandris ryng,
Our land ftud thre zer defolate but King, 1325
Kepyt full weyll at concord in gud ftait;
Throuch twa clemyt, yar hapnyt gret debait,
So ernyftfully, accord yaim nocht yai can;
Zour King yai aft for to be yair ourman;
Slcly he flaid throw ye ftrenthis off Scotland, 1330

Ye

Ye kynryk fyne he tuk in hys awne hand;
He maid a kyng agayne our rychtwyfs law,
For he off hym fuld hald ye regioun aw:
Contrar yis band was all ye haill barnage, 1335
For Scotland was zeit neuir into thrillage.
Gret Julius, yat tribut gat off all,
Hys wynnyng was in Scotland bot full fmall.
Yan your fals King, undyr colour but mar,
Throuch band he maid till Bruce yat is our ayr,
Throuch all Scotland with gret power yai raid, 1340
Undyr yat King quhilk he befor had maid;
To Bruce fen fyne he kepit na connand,
He faid, he wald nocht go and conquefs land
Till oyir men; and yus ye cafs befell.
Yan Scotland throuch he demayned hymfell; 1345
Slew our elderis, gret pete was to fe,
In pryfoune fyne lang tyme yai pynyt me,
Quhill I fra yaim was caftyn out for ded;
Thankyt be God he fend me fum remed.
Wengyt to be I prowyt all my mycht, 1350
Feill off yair kyn to dede fyn I haiff dycht.
Ye rage off youth gert me defyr a wyff,
Yat rewit I fayr and will do all my lyff;
A tratour knycht, but mercy gert hyr de,
Ane Hefylryg bot for defpyt off me. 1355
Yan rang I furth in cruell wer and payn,
Quhill we redemyt part off our land agayn.
Yan your curft King defyryt off us a trew,
Quhilk maid Scotland full rathly for to rew,
Into yat pefs yai fett a fattell Ayr, 1360
Yan

Yan auchtand fcor to dede yai hangyt yar,
At noblis war, and worthi off renoûne,
Off cot armys eldeft in yat regioune;
Yair dede we think to wenge in all our mycht.
Ye woman als, yat dulfully was dycht,   1365
Out off my mynd yat dede will neuir byd,
Quhill God me tak fra yis fals warld fa wyd;
Off Sothroune fen I can no pete haiff,
Zour men in wer I think neuir mar to faiff.
Ye breicht ters, was gret payn to behald,   1370
Bryft fra hys eyn, be he hys taill had tald.
Ye Queyn wepyt for pete off Wallace,
Allace, fche faid, wa worth ye curffyt cace,
In waryit tym yat Hefilryg was born,
Mony worthi throuch hys deid ar forlorn;   1375
He fuld haiff payne, yat faikles fic ane fleuch,
Ingland fen fyne has bouch it der enewch,
Thocht fche had beyne a Queyn or a Prynface.
Madeym, he faid, as God gyff me gud Grace,
Intill hyr tyme fche was als der to me,   1380
Prynface or Queyn, in quhat ftait fa yai be.
Wallace, fche faid, off yis talk we will cefs,
Ye mendis heroff is gud prayer and pefs.
I grant, he faid, off me as now na mayr,
Yis is rycht nocht bot ekyng off our cayr.   1385
Ye Queyn fand weyll langage no thing hyr bet,
Sche trowit with gold yat he mycht be ourfet;
Thre thowfand pound off fyneft gold fo red,
Sche gert be brocht to Wallace in yat fted.
Madeym, he faid, na fic tribut we craiff,   1390

Anoyr

Anoyr mends we wald off Ingland haiff,
Or we raturn fra yis regioune agayn,
Off zour fals blud yat has our elders flayn;
For all ye gold, and riches ze in ryng,
Ze get no pefs, but defyr off your King. 1395
Quhen fche faw weill gold mycht hyr nocht releiff,
Sum part in fport fche thoucht hym for to preiff.
Wallace, fche faid, ze war clepyt my luff,
Mor baundounly I maid me for to pruff,
Traiftand yarfor your rancour for to flak, 1400
Me think ze fuld do fumthing for my faik.
Rycht wyfly he maid anfuer to ye Queyn,
Madeym, he faid, and verite war feyn,
Yat ze my luffyt, I awcht yow luff agayn,
Yir wordis ar all na thing bot in wayn; 1405
Sic luff as yat is nathing till awance,
To tak alak and fyne get na plefance.
In fpech off luff futtell ye Sothroune ar,
Ze can us mok, fuppofs ye fe na mar.
In London, fche faid, for zow I fuffryt blaym; 1410
Our cunfaill als will lauch when we cum haym;
So may yai fay, wemen ar ferfs off thocht,
To fek freindfchipe, and fyne can get rycht nocht.
Madeym, he faid, we wait how yow ar fend,
Ze trow we haiff bot litill for to fpend. 1415
Fyrft with your gold, for ze ar rych and wyfs.
Ze wald us blynd, fen Scotts ar fo nyfs;
Syne plefand wordis off yow and ladyis fayr,
As quha fuld dryff ye byrds till a fnar
With ye fmall pype, for it moft frefche will call; 1420
          Madeym,

Madeym, as zeit ze ma nocht tempt us all;
Gret part off gud is left amang our kyn,
In Ingland als we fynd enewch to wyn.
Abayffit fche was to mak anfuer hym till.
Der fchyr, fche faid, fen yis is at your will,   1425
Wer or pefs, quhat fo zow likis beft,
Lat your hie witt and gud cunfaill degeft.
Madeym, he faid, now fall ze undirftand
Ye refoune quhy yat I will mak na band;
With zow, ladyis, I can na trewis bynd,   1340
For your fals King hereftir fone wald fynd,
Quhen he faw tym to brak it at hys will,
And playnly fay, he granty nocht yartill;
Yan had we nayn bot ladyis to rapruff:
Yat fall he nocht, be God yat is abuff,   1435
Apon wemen I will na wer begyn,
On zow in faith no worfchip is to wyn:
All he haill pefs apon hymfelff he fall tak,
Off pefs or wer quhat hapnyt we to tak.
Ye Queyn grantyt hys anfuer fufficient,   1440
Sa dyd ye laiff in place yat war prefent;
Hys deliuerance yai held off gret awaill,
And ftark enewch to fchaw to yair cunfaill.
Wa was ye Queyn hyr trawaill helpyt nocht,
Ye gold fche tuk yat yai had with hyr brocht,   1445
On to ye oft rycht frely fche it gaiff,
Till euir ilk man yat lykit for till haiff:
Yo menftraillis, harrolds, fche delt haboundandle,
Befekand yaim hyr freynd at yai wald be.
Quhen Wallace faw ye fredom off ye Queyn,   1450

Sadly

Sadly, he faid, ye futh weyll has beyn feyn,
Wemen may tempt ye wyfeſt at is wrocht;
Zour gret gentrice it fall neuir be for nocht,
We aſſure our oſt fall muff na thing,
Quhill tym ze may fend meſſage fra your King. 1455
Gyff it be fa, yat he accord and we,
Yan for zour faik it fall ye bettir be:
Your harrolds als fall faiffly cum and ga,
For zour fredom we fall trowbill na ma.
Sche thankyt hym off hys grant mony fyfs, 1460
And all ye ladyis apon a gudly wyfs.
Glaidly yai drank, ye Queyn and gud Wallace,
Yir ladyis als, and lordis in yat place
Hyr leyff fche tuk without langar abaid,
Fyffe myile yat nycht fouth till a nonry raid. 1465
Apon ye morn till London paſſit yai,
In Weſtminſter, quhar at ye cunfaill lay.
Wallace anfuer fche gart fchaw te ye King,
It neds nocht hyr raherfs mar off yis thing.
Ye gret cummend yat fche to Wallace gaiff, 1470
Befor ye King, in prefens off ye laiff,
Till trew Scotts it fuld gretly applefs,
Yocht Inglifmen yaroff had littill efs;
Off worfchipp, wyt, manheid, and gouernans,
Off fredome, trewth, key off remembrans, 1475
Sche callyt hym yar into yair hye prefens,
Yocht contrar yaim he ftud at hys defens:
Sa Chyftaynelik, fche faid, as he is feyn,
Intill Ingland, I trow, has neuir beyn:
Wald ze off gold giff hym yis rewmys rent, 1480

Fra

Fra honour he will nocht turn hys entent.
Sufferyt we ar, quhill ʒe may meſſage mak
Off wyſs lordis ſum part I reid yow tak,
To purcheſs peſs, withoutyn wordis mar,
For all Ingland may rew hys raid full ſayr.   1485
Ʒour haroldis als to paſs to hym has leyff,
In all hys oſt ʒar ſall na man ʒaim greyff.
Yan thankyt ʒai ye Queyn for hyr trawaill,
Ye King, and Lordis ʒat was off hys cunſaill.
Off hyr anſuer ye King appleſyt was;   1490
Yan thre gret Lords ʒai ordand for to paſs.
Yar cunſaill haill has found it was ye beſt,
Trewis to tak, or ellis ʒai get na reſt.
A harrold went, in all ye haiſt he may,
Till Tawbane waill, quhar at ye Scotts lay,   1495
Condeyt to haiff, quhill ʒai haiff ſaid ʒar will.
Ye cunſaill ſone condeyt gaiff hym till.
Agayne he paſt with Souerance till hys King.
Yan cheſyt ʒai thre Lords for yis thing.
Ye keyn Clyffurd, was yan ʒair Wardane haill,   1500
Bewmont, Wodſtok, all men off mekill waill:
Quhat yir thre wrocht ye laiff ſuld ſtand ʒar till,
Ye Kyngis ſeyll was gyffyn ʒaim at ʒair will.
Sone ʒai war brocht to ſpekyng to Wallace.
Wodſtok hym ſchawit mony ſuttell cace.   1505
Wallace he herd ye ſophammis euir ilk deill,
As ʒeit, he ſaid, me think ye mein bot weill;
In wrang ʒe hald, and dois us gret owtrage:
Off houſſis part ʒat is our heretage,
Owt off yis peſs in playn I mak ʒaim knawin,   1510
                                         Yaim

Yaim for to wyn, fen yat yai ar our awin;
Roxburch, Berweik, at owrs lang tym haiff beyn
Into ye handis off yon fals Southroune keyn,
We afk her als, be wertu off yis band,
Our ayrs, our King, be wrang led off Scotland; 1515
We fall yaim haiff, withoutyn wordis mar.
Till hys defyr ye Lordis grants yar;
For na kyn thing ye pefs yai wald nocht faill.
Ye zong Randell, at yan in London was,
Ye Lord off Lorn in yis band he can afs; 1520
Erle off Bowchane, but yan in tendyr age,
Eftir he grew a man off hycht, wyfs and large.
Cummyn and Soullis he gert deliuer als,
Quhilk eftir was till King Robert full fals.
Wallang fled our, and durft nocht byde yat mute,
In Pykardtc als till hym was na bute:
Bot Wallace wald erar haff had ye fals knycht,
Yan ten thoufand off fyneft gold fo brycht.
Ye Bruce he afkyt, bot he was had away,
Befor yat tym, to Calyfs, mony day; 1530
King Edwarde prowyt yat yai mycht nocht hym get,
Off Glofeftir hys uncle had hym fet,
At Calyfs yan had haly in kepyng.
Wallace yat tym gat nocht hys rychtwyfs King.
Ye Erle Patrik fra London alfua fend, 1539
Wycht Wallace to mak, as weill befor was kend,
Off hys mater a fynaill gouernance,
Till King Edwarde gaiff up hys legeance,
And tuk till hald off Scotland euirmar.
With full glaid hart Wallace reffawit hym yar; 1540

Yai honouryt hym rycht reuerendly as Lord.
Ye Scotts war all reiofyt off yat conford.
A hundreth horfs, with zong Lordis off renoune,
Till Wallace com, fred owt off yat prefoune.
Undyr hys feill King Edwarde yaim gert fend, 1545
For till gyff our, and mak a finaill end,
Roxburch, Berweik, quhilk is off mekill waill,
To Scottfmen, and all ye boundis haill.
To fyffe zer trews yai promyft be yair band.
Yan Wallace faid, we will pafs ner Scotland, 1550
Or ocht be feld; and yarfor mak us bown
Agayne we will befyd Northallyrtoun,
Quhar King Edwarde fyrft battaill hecht to me,
As it began, yar fall it endyt be.
Gret weyll zour Queyn, he chargyt ye meffage, 1555
It is for hyr yat we leyff our wiage.
A day he fet, quhen he fuld meit hym yar,
And feill yis pefs, withoutyn wordis mar.
Apon ye morn ye oft, but mar awyfs,
Trauountyt north apon a gudlye wyfs, 1560
To ye fet tryft yat Wallace had yaim maid.
Ye Inglis meffage come but mar abaid;
Yai feyllyt ye pefs withoutyn langar delay.
Ye meffage yan apon ye fecund day,
Till London went in all ye haift yai can. 1565
Ye worthi Scotts, with mony gudly man,
Till Bamburch com with all ye power haill,
Sexte thoufand, all Scotts off gret waill,
Ten dayis befor all Halow-ewyn yai fur;
On Lammefs day yai lycht on Caram mur, 1570

Yar

Yar lugyt yai with plefance as yai mocht,
Quhill on ye morn yat preifts to yaim focht,
In Caram kyrk, and feffyt in hys hand
Roxburch keyis, as yai had maid cummaund,
And Berweik als, quhilk Sothroune had fa lang; 1575
Yai frede ye folk in Ingland for to gang.
Fra yair lyffs ufchyt off ayir place,
Yai durft nocht weill byd rekynnyng off Wallace.
Captayne he maid, in Berweik off renoun,
Yat worthi was, gud Cryftell off Cetoun. 1580
Kepar he left till Roxburch Caftell wycht,
Schyr Jhon Ramfay, a wyfs and worthi knycht;
Syne Wallace felff, with Erle Patrik in playn,
To Dunbar raid, and reftoryt hym agayne,
In hys Caftell, and all yat heretage, 1585
With ye confent off all yat haill barnage.
Quhen Wallace was agreit and yis Lord,
To rewll ye rewm he maid hym gudly ford.
Scotland atour, fra Rofs to Solway fand,
He raid it thryfs, and ftatut all ye land. 1590
In ye Leyn-houfs a quhill he maid repayr,
Schyr Jhon Menteth yat tyme was Captayne yar,
Twyfs befor he had hys goffep beyn,
Bot na freindfchipe betwix yaim fyn was feyn.
Twa monethis ftill he duelt in Dimbertane; 1595
A houfs he foundyt apon ye rock off ftayne;
Men left he yar till byggyt to ye hycht,
Syn to ye march agayn he rydis rycht.
Into Roxburch yai chefyt hym a place,
A gud tour yar he gert byg in fchort fpace. 1600

Ye.

Ye kynrik ſtud in gud worſchip and eſs,
Was nayn ſa gret durſt hys nychtbour diſpleſs.
Ye abill ground gert lawbour thryftely,
Wittaill and froyte yar grew aboundanly.
Was neuir befor, ſen yis was callyt Scotland,   1605
Sic welth and peſs at anys in ye land.
He ſent Jop twyſs to Bruce in Huntyngtoune,
Beſekand hym to cum and tak hys croun.
Counſaill he tuk at fals Saxonis, allace!
He had neuir hap in lyff to get Wallace.   1610
Thre zer as yus ye rewm ſtud in gud peſs,
Off yis I mak my wordis for to ceſs,
And furthyr furth off Wallace I will tell,
Intill hys lyff quhat awentur zeit fell.
A Ryoll King yan ryngyt into France,   1615
Gret worſchip herd off Wallace gouernance,
Off prowis, pryſs, and off hys worthy deid,
And forthwart, fayr, commendede off manheid,
Bathe humyll, leyll, and off hys priwyt pryſs,
Off honour, trewth, and woid off cowatyſs.   1620
Ye nobill King, ryngand in ryolte,
Had gret delyte yis Wallace for to ſe,
And knew rycht weyll ſchortly to undirſtand
Ye gret ſuppryſs and ourſet off Ingland;
Als marweld he off Wallace ſmall power,   1625
Yat bot a King tuk ſic a rewme to ſter,
Agayn Ingland and gert yair malice ceſs,
Quhill yai deſyryt, with gud will to mak peſs.
And rycht onon a harrold gert he call,
In ſchort termys he has reherſyt all   1630

Off

Off hys entent completely till ane end,
Syne in Scotland he had hym for to wend;
And yus he wrait intill gret honour,
To Wilzham Wallace as a conquerour.
" O Lowit Leid with worschipe wyfs and wycht, 1635
" Yow werray help in haldyn off ye rycht,
" Yow rycht restorer off yi natyff land,
" With Godds Grace agayne yi fayis to stand
" In yi defens, helpar off rychtwyfs blud,
" O worthi berth, and blyssyt be yi fud; 1640
" As it is red in prophecy beforn,
" In happy tym for Scotland yow was born;
" I ye besek, with all humylite,
" My closs lettir yow wald consaiff and se,
" As your brodyr, I cryftyn King off France, 1645
" To ye berer ye her and gyff credance."
Ye herrold bownd, hym and to ye schip is gon
In Scotland sone he cummyn is onon;
Bot herrold lyk he sekys hys presens.
On land he went, and maid no residens 1650
In ony sted, quhar he presumyt yar,
So on a day he fand hym into Ayr,
In gud affer, and manlik cumpany.
Ye harrold yan, with honour reuerendly,
Has salust hym apon a gudly maner. 1655
And he agayn, with humyl hamly cher,
Resawit hym into rycht gudly wyfs.
Ye harrold yan, with worschip to deuifs,
Betuk till hym ye Kings wrytt off France.
Wallace on kne, with lawly obeyfance, 1660

Rycht

Rycht reuerendly, for worfchip off Scotland.
Quhen he it red, and had it undirftand,
At yis herrold he afkyt hys credence,
With afpre fpech, and manly contenence.
And he hym tald, as I haiff faid befor,   1665
Ye Kyngis defyr, quhat nedis wordis mor.
Ye hye honour, and ye gret nobilnes
Off your manheid, weyll knawyn in mony place,
Hym likis als weill your worfchipe till awance,
As ze war born a liege man off France;   1670
Sen hys regioun is flour off rewmys feyn,
Als ye gret bond off kindnes yow betweyn,
It war worfchip hys prefens for to fe,
Sen at yis rewme ftandis in fic degre.
Wallace confawyit, withoutyn taryng,   1975
Ye gret defyr off hys gud nobill King;
Syn till hym faid, as God off Hewyn me faiff,
Hereftir fone ze fall ane anfuer haiff
Off your defyr, yat ze haiff fchawit me till,
Welcum ze ar with a fre hartly will.   1680
Ye harrold baid, on to ye twentyeth day,
With Wallace ftill, in gud weillfayr and play,
Confumd ye tyme with worfchip and plefance,
Be gud awyfs maid hys deliuerance;
With hys awne hand he wrait on to ye King   1685
All hys entent, as twyching to yis thing.
Rycht rych reward he gaiff ye herrold to,
And hym conweyde quhen he had leiff to go,
Out off ye town with gudly cumpany;
Hys leyff he tuk, fyne went on to ye fe.   1690

Gud

Gud Wallace yan has maid hys prouidance,
Hys purpofs was to fe ye King off France,
Treft in wer to Santt Jhonftoune couth fayr,
A cunfaill yan he had gart ordand yar.
Intill hys fted he cheffyt a Gouernour   1695
To kep ye land, a man off gret walour,
Jamys gud Lord ye Stewart off Scotland,
Quhilk fadyr was as ftorys ber on hand,
To gud Waltir yat was off hye perage,
Ye Bruce fyne gat in mariage.   1700
Yaroff to fpek as now I haiff no fpace,
It is weyll knawin, thankyt be Godds grace.
And to ye harrold, withoutyn refidens.
Quho he approchyt to ye Kingis prefens.
Fra ye Rochell ye land fone has he tayn,   1705
Atour ye lands he graithit hym to gayn,
Sekand ye King, als gudly as he may;
So to ye court he paffyt on a day,
To Paryfs went, was peirles off renoun,
Ye King yat tyme held palace in yat toun.   1710
Quhen he hym faw, graithly has undirftand,
He fperyt tithings, and weyllfayr off Scotland.
Ye harrold faid, into yir termys fchort,
Yat all was gud; he had ye mar comfort.
Saw yow Wallace, yat Chyftayne off yat land?   1715
And he faid, za, yat I dar tak on hand,
A worthyar yis day lyffand is nayn,
In way off wer, als fer as I haiff gayn.
Ye hie worfchip, and ye gret nobilnes,
Ye gud weyllfayr, plefande and worthines,   1720
Ye

Ye rych reward was mychty for to fe,
Yat for your faik he kythyt apon me;
And hys anfuer in wrytt he has zow fend.
Ye King refawit it with a lycht attend,
Yis hie affect and dyt off hys wrytyng.   1725
" O Ryoll Roy, and rychtwyfs crownyt King,
" Yow knaw yis weill, be oyir ma yan me,
" Quhow yat our rewlm ftandis in perplexite.
" Ye fals natioun, yat we ar nychtbours to,
" Quhen pleffis yaim, yai mak us ay ado;   1730
" Yar may na band be maid fufficians,
" Bot ay in it yai fynd a warians.
" To wait a tyme, quhill God yat it may be,
" Within a zer I fall your prefens fe."
Off yis anfuer weill plefyt was ye King.   1735
Leyff I hym yus in ryolte to ryng,
And glaid comfort rycht as I haiff zow tald,
Off Wallace forth I will my procefs hald.

    EXPLICIT LIBER OCTAUUS
    ET INCIPIT NONUS.

THE LIFE OF SIR WILLIAM WALLACE, &c.

BOOK IX.

Wallace Fights the Red Reaver—Gets his Pardon from the French King—Paſſes to Guenne to Fight the Engliſh—King Edward invades Scotland—Wallace Returns.

IN Aprill ye ane and twenty day,
  Ye hie calend, yus cancer, as we ſay,
Ye luſty tym off Mayus freſche cummyng,
Celeſtiall gret blythnes in to bryng;
Pryncypaill moneth forſuth it may be ſeyn,   5
Ye Hewynly hewis apon ye tendyr greyne.
Quhen ald ſaturn hys cloudy courſs had gon,
Ye quhilk had beyn baith beſt and burdis bon.
Zepherus ek, with hys ſwete vapour,
He confort has be wyrkyng off natour,   10
All fruttuouſs thing intill ye erd adoun,
Att rewllyt is undyr he yie regioun.
Sobyr Luna, in flowyng off ye ſe,
Quhen brycht Phebs is in hys chemage.
Ye bulys courſs ſo takin had hys place,   15

And

And Jupiter was in ye crawis face.
Quhen aryes, yat hot fyng coloryk,
Into ye ram quhilk had hys rowmys ryk,
He chofyn had hys place and hys manfioun, 20
In Capricorn, ye fyng off ye Lyoun.
Gentill Jupiter, with hys myld ordinance,
Bathe erb and tre reuerts in plefance;
And frefche Flora hyr flowry mantill fpreid,
In euery waill, bathe hop, hycht, and meide. 25
Yis famyn tyme, for yus myne auctor fayis,
Wallace to pafs off Scotland tuk hys wayis;
Be fchort awifs he fchup hym to ye fe,
And fyfte men tuk in hys cumpane.
He leit no word yan walk off hys paffage,
Or Inglifmen had ftoppyt hym hys wiage: 30
Nor tuk na leiff at ye lordis off ye parlyment,
He wyft full weyll yai wald nocht all confent,
To fuffyr hym out off ye land to go;
For yi onon, withoutyn wordis mo,
He gart forfe, and ordand weill hys fchip, 35
And yir war part paft in hys falowfchip;
Twa Wallace was hys kynnys men full ner,
Craufurd, Kneland was haldyn till hym der.
Off Kyrkcubre he purpoft hys paffage,
Semen he feyt and gaiff yaim gudlye wage; 40
Yai wantyt nocht off wyn, wittaill nor ger,
A fayr new barge rycht worthi wrocht for wer;
With yat yai war a gudlye cumpany,
Off waillit men had wrocht full hardely.
Bonalais drank rycht glaidly in a morow, 45

Syn

Syn leiff yai tuk, and with Santt Jhon to borow.
Botts was fchot, and fra ye rock yaim fent,
With glaid harts, at anys in yai went;
Apon ye fchip yai rowit haftely.
Ye feymen yan walkand full befyly,   50
Ankyrs wand in wyfly on ayir fyd,
Yair lynys keft and waytyt weill ye tyd;
Leit falys fall, and has yair courfs ynom,
A gud gay wynd out off ye rycht art com.
Freiks in forftarne rewlit weill yair ger,   55.
Ledys on luff burd, with a lord lik fer.
Lanfys laid out, to yar paffage found.
With full fayll yus fra Scotland furth yai found,
Salyt our ye day and als ye nycht,
Apon ye morn, quhen ye fon raifs brycht,   65
Ye fhipmafter on to ye top he went,
South-eft he faw, yat trublyt hys entent,
Sexteyn falis arayit all on raw,
In colour reid, and towart hym couth draw.
Ye glyttyrand fone apon yaim fchawit brycht,   65
Ye fe about enlumynyt with ye lycht.
Yis mannys fpreit was in ane extafy,
Doun went he fone, and faid full forowfully,
Allace, quoth he, ye day yat I was born,
Without rameid our lywys ar forlorn,   70
In curfyt tym I tuk yis cur on hand;
Ye beft Chyftayne, and refkew off Scotland,
Our raklefly I haiff tayn apon me,
With waik power to bryng hym throw ye fe;
A forfyt nocht, wald God I war torment,   75

Sa Wallace mycht with worfchip chaip unfehent.
Quhen Wallace faw, and hard yis mannys mon,
To confort hym in gud will is he gon.
Maifter, he faid, quhat has amowit ze?
Not for myfelff, yis man faid petuifle, 80
Bot off a thing I dar weill undirtane,
Yocht all war her ye fchippis of braid Bertane,
Part fuld we lofs, fet fortoun had it fuorn,
Ye beft wer man in fe is us beforn,
Leffand yis day, and king is off ye fc. 85
Wallace fone fperd, wait you quhat he may be?
Ye Rede Reffayr, yai call hym in his ftill,
Yat I hym faw euyr, waryt worth yat quhill;
For myn awn lyff I wald na murnyng mak,
Is na man born yat zon tyran will tak. 90
He favis nayn, for gold, nor oyir gud,
Bot flayis and drownis all derfly in ye flud,
He gets na grace, thocht he war kyng or knycht,
Yir fexteyn zer he has doyn gret unrycht.
Ye power is fa ftrang he has to fter, 95
May nayn efchaip yat cummys in hys danger.
Wald we hym burd, na but is to begyn,
Ye lakeft fchip yat is hys flote within
May fayll us doun on to a dulfull ded.
Yan Wallace faid, fen zou can na ramed, 100
Tell me hys feyr, and how I fall hym knaw,
Quhat is hys oyfs, and fyne go luge ze law.
Ye fchipman fayis, rycht weill I may hym ken,
Throuch graith takynnys, full clerly he hys men,
Hys cot armour is feyn in mony fteid, 105

Ay

Ay battaill boun, and rewell ay off reid;
Yis formaift fchip, yat perfewis zow fa faft,
Hymfelf is in, he will nocht be agaft;
He will zow hayll quhen yat he cummys zow ner,
Without tary yan mon ze ftryk on fter;   110
Hymfelf will entir fyrft full hardely,
Yir ar ye fyngnys yat ye fall knaw hym by;
A bar off blew intill hys fchenand fcheild,
A bend off greyn defyren ay ye feild;
Ye rede betakannys blud and hardyment,   115
Ye greyn, curage, encreffand hys entent;
Ye blew he bers, becaufs he is a Cryftyn man,
Sadly agayn Wallace anfuerd yan,
Thocht he be cryftynyt, yis war na Godlyk deid,
Go undyr loft, Santt Androw mot us fpeid.   120
Bathe fchipmaftir, and ye fterman alfo,
In ye holl, but baid, he gert yaim go.
Hys fyftye men withoutyn langar reft,
Wallace gart ray into yair armour preft,
Fourty and aucht on luff burd laid yaim law;   125
Wilzham Crawfurd yan till hym gert he caw,
And faid, yow can fum part off fchipman fair,
Yi oyfs has beyn oft in ye toune off Ayr,
I pray yow tak yis doctryn off me,
Luk yat yow ftand ftrekly be yis tre,   130
Quhen I byd ftryk, to fcheruice be yow bane,
Quhen I ze warn latt draw ye faill agane.
Kneland, cufyng, cum tak ze fter on hand,
Her on ye waill ner by ye I fall ftand,
God gyd our fchip, as now I fay na mar.   135

Ye barge, be yat, with a fu'l warlik far,
Hymfelff on loft with a drawyn fuerd,
And bad hys fterman lay yaim langs ye bourd;
On loude he cryit, ftryk, doggs fe fall de.
Crawfurd leit draw ye fayll a litill we. 140
Ye Captayne fone lap in and wald nocht ftynt.
Wallace on haift be ye gorgyt hym hynt,
On ye our loft keft hym quhar he ftud,
Quhill neyfs and mouth all rufchyt out off blud;
A forgyt knyff, but baid, he brads out. 145
Ye wer fchippis was lappyt yaim about.
Ye mekill barge had nocht yaim clyppyt faft,
Crawfurd drew faill, fkewyt by, and off yaim paft.
Ye Reiffar cryt, with petous woice and cler,
Grace off hys lyff, for hym yat boucht yow der; 150
Mercy, he faid, for hym yat dyit on rud,
Layfer to mend, I haiff fpilt mekill blud,
For my trefpas I wald mak fum ramed.
Wallace wyft weill, yocht he war brocht to ded,
And off hys lyff fum refkew mycht he mak, 155
A bettir purpofs fone he can to tak;
And als he rewyt hym, for hys lyff was ill,
In Latyn tong rycht yus he faid hym till,
I tuk neuir man, yat enemy was to me,
For Godds faik yi lyff I grant to ye. 160
Bathe knyff and fuerd he tuk fra hym onon,
Up be ye hand and as prifouner has hym ton,
And on hys fuerd fchárplye he gert hym fuer,
Fra yat day furth he fuld hym neuyr der.
Commaund yi men, quoth Wallace, till our pefs, 165

Yat

Yat fchot off gown, yat was nocht eith to cefs;
Ye caft it was rycht awfull on ayir fyd.
Ye Rede Reiffar commaundyt yaim to byd,
Held out a gluff, in takyn off ye trew.
Hys men beheld, and fone yat fenze knew, 170
Left off yair fchott, yat fygn quhen yat yai faw,
Hys grettaft barge towart hym he couth draw;
Lat be zour wer, yir ar our freyndis at ane,
I traift to God our werft dayis ar gane.
He aft Wallace to do quhat was hys will. 175
With fchort awifs rycht yus he faid hym till,
For Inglifmen I wait nocht quhat may aill,
For yar, God will, is our purpofs to be,
Skour weyll about for fcoukars in ye fe.
Hys cummaund yai did in all ye haift yai can. 180
Wallace defyryt to tak mor with yis man,
Sadly he fperd, off quhat land was zow born?
Off France, quoth he, and my elders beforn,
And yar we had fum part off heretage,
Zet fers fortoun yus brocht me in a rage. 185
Wallace fperd, how com you into yis lyff?
Forfuth, he faid, bot throuch a fudan ftryff,
So hapnyt me into ye kings prefens,
Our raklefly to do our gret offens;
A nobill man, off gud fame and renoune, 190
Yat throw my deid was put to confufioune,
Dede off a ftraik, quhat nedis wordis mor;
All helpyt nocht, yocht I repentyt full for.
Throw freyndis off ye court I chapyt off yat place,
And neuir fen fyne couth get ye kings grace: 195

For my faik mony off my kyn gert yai de.
And quhen I faw it mycht no bettir be,
Bot leiff ye land yat me behuffyt o neid,
Apon a day to Burdeous I zeid;
Ane Inglis fchip fa gat I on a nycht, 200
For fey lawbour yat ernyftfully was dycht;
To me yar femblyt mifdears and weill mo,
And in fchort tym we multyplyt fo,
Yat yar war few our power mycht withftand.
In tyrranny yus haiff we rongyn lang. 205
Yis fexteyn zer I haiff beyn on ye fe,
And doyn gret harm yarfor full wais me.
I fawit nayn, for gold nor gret ranfoun,
Bot flew and drownyt into ye fe adoun.
Fawour I did to folk off fynday land, 210
Bot Franchmen na freyndfchip with me fand,
Yai gat na grace als for as I mycht ryng;
Als on ye fe I clypyt was a king.
Now fee I weyll yat my fortoun is went,
Wincuft with ane yat gars me fair rapent. 215
Quha wald haiff faid, yis famyn day at morn,
I fuld with ane yus lychtly doun be born,
In gret hething my men it wald haiff tane;
Myfelff trowit till machit mony ane:
Bot I haiff found ye werray playn contrar, 220
Her I gyff our roubry for euirmar;
In fic myfrewll I fall neuir armes ber,
Bot gyff it be in honeft oyfs to wer.
Now haiff I tald yow part off my blyfs and payn,
For Godds faik fum kyndnes kyth agayn, 225

My

My hart will brek bot I wait quhat yow be,
Yus outrageoufly yat has rabutyt me;
For weill I wend yat leffand had beyn nane,
Be forfs off ftrenth mycht me as prifonour tane,
Except Wallace, yat has rademyt Scotland, 230
Ye beft is callyt yis day beltyt with brand;
Intill hys wer war worfchip for to wak,
As now in warld I trew he has no mak.
Yarat he fmylyt, and faid, freind, weill, may be
Scotland had myft off mony fic as he. 235
Quhat is yi nayme, tell me, fa haiff yow feill.
Forfuth, he faid, Thomas off Longoweill.
Weyll bruk zow it, all yus ftynts our ftryff,
Schaip to pleyfs God in mendyng off yi lyff;
Yi faithfull freind myfelff thinkis to be, 240
And als my nayme I fall fone tell to ze;
For chans off wer you fuld na murnyng mak,
As werd will wyrk, yi fortoun mon zow tak;
I am yat man yat you awanfs fa hie,
And bot fchort tyme fen I come to ye fe; 245
Off Scotland born, my rycht nayme is Wallace.
On kneis he fell, and thankyt God off Grace;
I dar awow, yat zoldyn is my hand,
To ye beft man yat belts hym with brand.
Forfuth, he faid, yis blythis me mekill mor, 250
Yan off Floryng ze gaiff me fexty fcor.
Wallace anfuerd, fen yow ar her throw chance,
My purpofs is be yis wiage in France;
And to ye king, fen I am boun to pafs,
To my reward yi pefs I think to afs. 255

Pefs I wald haiff off my rychtwyfs king,
And na langar into yat realm to ryng,
Yar to tak lyff, and cum off it agayn,
In yi feruice I think for to remayn.
Seruice, he faid, Thomas yat may nocht be, 260
Bot gud freyndfchip, as I defyr off ye.
Gert draw ye wyn, and ilk man mery maid,
Be yis ye fchippis was in ye Rochell raid.
Ye rede blafonys yai had born into wer,
Ye toune was fone intill a fudane fer. 265
Ye Rede Reiffar yai faw was at yair hand,
Ye quhilk throw ftrenth mycht nane agyn hym ftand.
Sum fchippis fled, and fum ye land has tayn,
Clariównys blew, and trumpatts mony ane.
Quhen Wallace faw ye pepill was on fter, 270
He gaiff commaund na fchip fuld ner apper,
Bot hys awin barge into ye hawyn gart draw.
Ye folk was fayn quhen yai yat fenze faw;
Rycht weill yai knew in gold ye red lyoun,
Leit up ye port, refawit hym in ye toun, 275
And fufferyt yaim, for all yat he had brocht.
Ye rede nawyn into yai hawyn yai focht,
On land yai went, quhar yai lykyt to pafs.
Rycht few yar wyft quhat Scottfinan Wallace was;
Bot weyll yai thocht he was a gudly man, 280
And honoryt hym in all ye craft yai can.
Bot four dayis ftill Wallace ramaynyt yar,
Yir men he callyt, quhen he was boun to fair,
He yaim cummandyt apon yat coft to byd,
Quhill he yaim fred for chans at mycht betyd; 285
Ber

Ber yow ewyn, quhat gud yat euir ye spend,
Leiff on your awne, quhill tithands I you send;
Gar fell zour schippis, and mak yow men off pess,
It war gud tym off wykkitness to cess;
Your Captane sall pass to ye King with me,   290
Throw help of God I sall hys warrand be.
He gart graith hym in soit with hys awin men,
Was no man yar yat mycht weyll Thomas ken;
Lykly he was, manlik off contenance,
Lik to ye Scotts, be mekill gowernance,   295
Saiff off hys tong, for Inglis had he nane,
In Latyn weill he mycht suffice for ane.
Yus past hys court in all ye haist yai may.
To Parys toun yai went apon a day.
Tythings was brocht off Wallace to ye king,   300
So gret defyr he had off na kyn thing,
As in yat tym, quhill he had feyn Wallace,
To meyt hymfelff he waytyt apon cace,
In a gardyng, quhar he gart yaim be brocht.
Till hys prefens with manly feyr yai focht,   305
Twa and fyfte at anys kneland doun,
And saluft hym as ryoll off maift renoun,
With rewllyt spech in sa gudly awyss,
All Franse couth nocht nuortour yan dewyss.
Ye Queyn had leiff, and com into hyr effer,   310
For mekill fche herd off Wallace deid in wer.
Quhat nedis mor off curtassy to tell,
Yai kepyt weyll yat to ye Scotts befell.
Off Kings fer I dar mak no rahers,
My febill mynd, my trublyt spreit rewers;   315

Off

Off rych feruice, quhat nedis wordis mar,
Mycht non be found bot it was prefent yar.
Sone eftir meit ye king to parlour went,
With gudly lords, yar Wallace was prefent.
Yan commound yai off mony fundry thing,   320
To fpek with hym gret defyr had ye king.
At hym he fperyt off wer ye gowernance.
He anfuerd hym, with manly contenance,
Till euery poynt, als fer as he had feill,
In Latyn tong rycht naturally and weill.   325
Ye king confawit, fone throw hys hie knawlage,
Quhat wermen oyffyt be reyff in yar paffage,
Intill hys mynd ye Rede Reiffar yan was,
Merwell he had quhow he leit Wallace pafs.
Till hym he faid, it war fumthing to blaym,   330
Ze mycht haiff fend, be our herrold fra haym,
Eftir power, to bryng yow throw ye fe.
God thank yow, fchyr, enewch yaroff had we,
Feill men may pafs, quhar yai fynd na perill;
Rycht few may kep, quhar nayn is to affaill.   335
Wallace, he faid, yaroff merwell haiff I,
A tyrand ryngs, in ire full cruelly,
Apon ye fe yat gret forow has wrocht,
Mycht we hym get it fuld not be for nocht;
Born off yis land, a natyff man to me,   340
Yarfor on us ye grettar harme dois he.
Yan Thomas quok, and changyt contenans,
He hard ye king hys ewyll deds ewans.
Wallace beheld, and fenzeit in a part,
Forfuth, he faid, we fand nane in yat art,   345
Yat

Yat profyrryt us fic unkindlynes;
Bot with zour leiff I fpek in haymlynes,
Trow ze be fycht ye couth yat fquier knaw?
Till lang it war fen tym yat I hym faw;
Bot yir words off hym ar bot in wayn, 350
Or he com her rycht gud men will be flayn.
Yan Wallace faid, her I haiff broucht with me,
Off likly men yat was in our countre,
Quhilk off all yir wald ze call hym moft lyk.
Amang yaim blent yat ryoll Roy moft ryk, 355
Wefyt yaim weill, baith ftatur and curage,
Maner, makdome, yair faffoun and yair wefage;
Sadly he faid, awyfit fobyrly,
Yat largeft man, quhilk ftandis next yow by,
Wald I call hym, be makdome to dewice, 360
Yir ar nothing bot wordis off office.
Befor ye king on kneis fell gud Wallace.
O Royll Roy, off hie honour and grace,
With waift wordis I will nocht you trawaill,
Now I will fpek fumthing for myne awaill. 365
Our barnat land has beyn ourfet with wer,
With Saxonis blud yat dois us mekill der,
Slayn our eldris, deftroyit our rychtwyfs blud,
Waiftit our realm off gold and oyir gud;
And ze ar her, in mycht and ryolte, 370
Yow fuld haiff ey till our aduerfite,
And us fupport, throw kyndnes off ye band,
Quhilk is confchyrwyt betwix yow and Scotland;
As I am her, at your charge, for plefance,
My lyflat is bot honeft chewyfance. 375

Flour

Flour off realmys forfuth is yis regioun,
To my reward I wald haiff gret gardoun.
Wallace, he faid, now afk quhat ze wald haiff.
Gud gold or land fall nocht be lang to craiff.
Wallace anfuerd, fo ze it grant to me   380
Quhat I wald haiff, it fall fone chofyn be.
Quhateuir ze afk, yat is in yis regioun,
Ze fall it haiff, except my wyff and ye croun.
He thankyt hym off hys gret kyndlynes.
My reward all fall be afkyng off grace,   385
Pefs to yis man I broucht with me throw chance,
Her I quyt cleyn all oyir gyfftis in France;
Yis famyn is he, gyff ze knaw hym weill,
Yat we off fpak, Thomas off Longaweill;
Be rygour ze defyryt he fuld be flayn,   390
I hym reftor into your grace agayn,
Refaiff hym fayr, as leige man off your land.
Ye king marweld, and couth in ftudy ftand,
Perfytly knew yat it was Longaweill,
He hym forgaiff hys trefpas euir ilk deill,   395
Bot for hys faik yat hyddyr brocht;
For gold or land, ellis he gat it nocht.
Wallace he faid, I had leuir off gud land,
Thre hundreth pund haiff fefyt in yi hand,
Yat I haiff faid fall be grantyt in plain,   400
Her I reftor Thomas to pefs agayn,
Derer to me yan euyr he was befor,
All for zour faik, yocht it war mekill mor:
Bot I wald wytt quhow yat merwell befell.
Wallace anfuerd, ye trewth I fall yow tell.   405
Yan

Yan he raherfyt quhat hapnyt on yat day,
As ze befor in my autor hard fay.
Quhen ye gud king had herd yis fudan cafs,
Apon ye fe ye forfycht off Wallace,
Ye king hym held rycht worthi till awans, 410
He faw in hym manheid and gouernans;
So did ye Queyn, and all yir oyir Lordis,
Ilk wycht off hym gret honour yan recordis.
He purcheft pefs, for all ye power haill,
Fyfteyn hundreth was left in ye Rochaill; 415
Gert cry yaim fre, trew fchyrwandis to ye king,
And neuir agayn fantyt in fic thing.
Quhen Thomas was reftoryt to hys rycht,
Off hys awin hand ye king has maid hym knycht.
Eftir he gaiff ftayt to hys nereft ayr, 420
And maid hymfelff with Wallace for to fayr.
Yus he was brocht fra naym off Reyff, throw cace,
Be fudand chans off hym and wycht Wallace.
Yus leyff I yaim in worfchipe and plefance,
At liking with ye gud king off France. 425
Yar threty dayis he lugyt into reft,
Sa to ramayn he thocht it nocht ye beft;
Still into pefs he couth nocht lang endur,
Uncorduall it was till hys natur.
Rycht weill he wyft Inglifmen occupyit 430
Guane yat tym, yarfor he has afpyit
Sum jeperte apon yaim for to mak.
A gudly leyff he at ye king couth tak.
Off Franchmen he wald nayne with hym call,
At ye fyrft tym for awentur mycht fall; 435
But

Bot Schyr Thomas yat feruice couth perfew,
He wyft nocht weill gyff all ye laiff was trew.
Off Scotts men yai femblyt haifty ely
Nyne hundreth fone off worthi chewalry.
In Gyan land full haiftely couth ryd, 440
Raiffyt feill fyr, and waiftyt wonnyngs wyd;
Fortrafs yai brak, and ftalwart byggyngs wan,
Derfly to dede brocht mony Sothroune man.
A werlik toune fa fand yai in yat land,
Quhilk Schenoun hecht, yat Inglifmen had in hand.
Towart yat fteid full fadly Wallace wrocht,
Be ony wyfs affailze gyff he mocht,
Bargane till haiff gyff he mycht get yaim out.
Get ftrenth off wode yat tyme was yar about;
Ye toun als ftud apon a wattir fyd. 450
Intill a park, yat was bath lang and wyd,
Yai bufchyt yaim, quhill paft was ye nycht.
Quhen ye fone raifs, four hundreth men he dycht;
Ye laiff he gert Crawford in bufchment tak,
Gyff yai myfterd, a refkew for to mak. 455
Yan Longaweill, yat ay was full fawage,
With Wallace paft, as ane to yat fcrymage.
Yir four hundreth rycht wondyr weill arayit,
Befor ye toune ye playn Baner difplayit.
Yis was not to yaim weyll knawyn in yat contre, 460
Ye lyoun in gold rycht awfull for to fe.
A forray keft, and fefyt mekill gud.
Wermen within, yat playnly undirftud,
Son ufhyt forth ye pray for to refkew.
Ye worthi Scotts ftill Inglifmen yai flew; 465

Ye

Ye laiff for dreid fled to ye toune agayn.
Ye forray tuk ye pray, and paſt ye playn,
Towart ye park bot power off ye toun,
Uſchyt agayn in awfull battaill boun,
A thouſand haill with men off armys ſtrang, 470
Few baid yarin yat mycht to Bargane gang.
Yan Wallace gert ye ferreours leyff ye pray,
Aſſemblyt ſone intill a gud aray.
A cruell counter at yat metyng was ſeyn,
Off wycht wer men into yair armour cleyn. 475
Feill loſſyt yair lyff apon ye Sothroune ſyd,
Bot nocht for yi rycht bauldly yai abyd.
Off ye Scotts part worthi men yai ſlew.
Wilzham Crawfurd, yat weyll ye perill knew,
Out off ye park he gert ye buſchement paſs, 480
Into ye feild quhar feyll men fechtand was,
At yair entre yai gart full mony de.
Ye Ingliſmen was wondyr laith to fle;
Full worthely yai wrocht into yat place,
Baid neuir ſa few ſo lang agayne Wallace, 485
With ſic power as he yat day was yar.
On ayir ſyd aſſailzeit ferly ſayr.
In to ye ſtour ſo felloumly yai wrocht,
Rycht worthi men derfly to dede yai brocht;
With poynts perſyt throch plats burnyſt brycht. 490
Wallace hymſelff, and gud Thomas knycht,
Quhom yat yai hyt maid neuir mar debait.
Ye Sothroune part was handlyt yar full hayt.
Into yat place yai mycht na langar byd,
Out off ye feild with ſar harts yai ryd; 495

On to ye toune yai fled full haiftely.
Wallace folowit, and hys gud chewalry,
Fechtand fo faft into yat thykkeft thrang,
Quhill in ye toun he entryt yaim amang;
With hym Crawfurd, and Longawcill off mycht,
And Rychard als, Wallace hys cufyng wycht ; 500
Fyfteyn yai war off Scotts cumpany,
Yus hapnyt yai amang ye gret party.
A cruell portar gat apon ye wall,
Powit out a pyn, ye portculys leit fall. 505
Inglifmen faw yat entryt was na ma,
Apon ye Scotts full hardely yai ga:
Bot till a wall yai haiff yair bakks fet,
Sad ftrakys and fayr bauldly about yaim fet.
Rychard Wallace ye turngreis weill has feyn, 510
He folowit faft apon ye portar keyn,
Atour ye wall deid in ye dyk hym draiff,
Tuk up ye port, and leit in all ye laiff.
Quhen Wallace men had yus ye entre won,
Full gret flawchtyr agayn yai haiff begon ; 515
Yai favit nayne apon ye Sothroune fyd,
Yat wappynys bar, or harnes in yat tyd ;
Wemen and barnys ye gud yai tuk yaim fra,
Syne gaiff yaim leyff into realm to ga;
And preyfts, als yat war nocht in ye feild : 520
Off agyt men, quhilk mycht na wappynys weild
Yai flew nayn fic, fo Wallace charge was,
Bot maid yaim fre, at yair large to pafs.
Ryches off gold yai gat in gret plente,
Harnes and horfs, yat mycht yaim weill fupple. 525

With

With Franch folk plenyſt ye toune agayn,
On ye tenth day ye feild yai tuk in playn;
Ye riwer doun into ye land yai focht,
On Sothroune men full mekill maiſter yai wrocht.
Quhen to ye king trew men had tald yis taill, 530
Off Frauchmen yai femblyt a battaill;
Twentye thoufand, lele leg's off France,
Hys broyir yaim led was Duk off Orleance;
Throw Gyan land in rayid battaill yai raid,
To folow Wallace, and maid bot litill baid 535
For Franch fupple, to help yaim in yair rycht,
Ner Burdeous, or yai ourtuk hym mycht,
Gud Wallace was, and Thomas had in playn;
For fum men tald, yat Burdeous with gret mayn,
Within fchort tym thoucht battaill for to gyff: 540
Bot fra yai wyſt yat Franch folk couth raleiff,
With gret power with helpyng off Wallace,
Uthyr purpofs yai tuk into fchort fpace.
In Pykarte fone meſſage yai couth fend,
Off Wallace com yai tauld it till ane end. 545
Off Glofyſtir, Captayne off Calyfs was,
Ye hardy Erle, and maid hym for to pafs
In Ingland fone, and fyne to London went,
Off Wallace deid he tald in ye parlyment.
Sum playnly, yat Wallace brak ye pefs. 550
Wyfs men faid, nay, and prayit yaim for to cefs.
Lord Bowmont faid he tuk bot for Scotland
And nocht for France, yat fall ze undyrſtand,
Gyff our indentour fpekis for ony mair,
He has doyn wrang, ye futh ye may declair. 555

Wodſtok anſuerd, ſchyr, ze haiff ſpokyn weill,
Bot contrar reſoune yat taill is euir ilk deill :
Gyff zow be he yat band for hym and hys,
May na man ſay bot he has wrocht amyſs,
For pryncipaly he band with us ye trew, 560
And now agayne begynnys a malice new.
Schyr, king, he ſaid, gyff ze think euir to mak
On Scotland wer, on hand now zow ſall tak,
Quhill he is out, or ellis it helpis nocht.
As Wodſtok ſaid, ye haill conſaill has wrocht; 565
Power yai rayſſit on Scotland for to ryd,
Be land and ſe yai wald na langar byd.
Yair land'oſt yai rayit weill in deid ;
Yair wantgard tuk ye hardy Erle to leid
Off Gloſyſtir, yat off wer had gret feill ; 570
Off Longcaſtell ye Duk demanyt weill
Ye mydillward ; on to ye ſe yai ſend
Schyr Jhone Sewart, yat weill ye north land kend.
Ye Knycht Wallang befor ye oſt in raid,
In ſic a way with ewyll Scotts men he maid, 575
Mony caſtells he gert ſone zoldin be
Till Ingliſmen, withoutyn mar melle.
Or ye beſt wyſt, yat it was wer in playn,
Schyr Jhon Sewart, yat com in be ye ſe,
Santt Jhonſtoune ſone gat be a jeperte. 580
Dunde yai tuk, and put Scottſmen to dede ;
In Fyff fra yaim was nocht kepyt a ſted ;
And all ye ſouth, fra Cheuyot to ye ſe ;
Into ye weſt yar mycht na ſuccour be ;
Ye worthi Lord, yat ſuld haiff gouernyt yis, 585
God

God had hym tayn, we trow in leſtand bliſs;
Hys ſon Waltir, yat bot a child yan was,
Trew men hym tuk, and couth in Arrane paſs.
Adam Wallace yan wyſt off no ſupple,
Till Rawchle went, and Lindſay off Cragge;   590
Gud Robert Boid maid no reſidens;
For haiſty deſait, yai tuk yaim to defens.
Schyr Jhon ye Grayme in Dundaff mycht not byd,
Succour he ſocht into ye foreſt off Clid.
Ye Knycht Sewart, a ſchirreff maid in Fyff   595
Schyr Amer Brim, and gaiff for term off lyff,
Ye lands haill yat Wallang aucht befor.
Richard Lundy had gret dreid off yair ſchoyr;
He likyt nocht for to cum to yair peſs,
For yis in Fyff yai wald nocht lat hym ceſs;   600
To paſs our Tay as yan it mycht nocht be,
For Ingliſmen ſo rewllyt yat cuntre
Out off ye land he ſtaw away be nycht,
Auchtand with hym yat worthi war and wycht;
And als hys ſone, yat was off tendyr cild,   605
Bot eftir ſone he couth weill wapynnys weild.
At Stirlyng Bryg, quharat ye wach was ſet,
Yar paſſyt he away withoutyn let.
In Dundaff mur Schyr Jhon ye Grayme he ſocht;
A woman tald as yan befor has wrocht;   610
And till a ſtrenth he drew hym on ye morn.
Laynrik was tayn with zong Thomas off Thorn,
Sa Lundy yar mycht mak na langar ramayn,
Be ſouth Tynto lugis yai maid in playn.
Schyr Jhon ye Grayme gat wyt yat he was yar,   615

Till

Till hym he paſt withoutyn wordis mar.
Wallang gart bryng fra Carlele cariage,
To ſtuff Bothwell with wyn and gud warnage.
Lundy and Grayme gat wytt off yat awaill,
Rycht ſudanly yai maid yaim till aſſaill;   620
Fyftye yai war off nobill chewalry,
Agayn four ſcor off Inglis cumpany.
Ane Skelton yan kepyt ye cariage,
A brankſtewat yat was hys heretage.
Lundy and Grayme met with ye ſquier wycht, 625
Feill Ingliſmen to dede derfly yai dycht.
Sexte was ſlayn apon ye toyir ſid,
And fyffe off Scotts, ſo bauldly yai abid.
Gret gud yai wan, bathe gold and oyir ger,
Wittayll and horſs yat hapnyt in yat wer.   630
Sen yai haiff ſeyn weill lang yai mycht not leſt
On to yat land, yarfor yai thocht it beſt,
To ſeik ſum place, in ſtrenth yat yai mycht bid,
For Sothroune men had plenyſt on ilk ſid.
Lundies luge yai left apon a nycht,   635
In ye Lennox ye way yai paſſyt rycht
Till Erle Malcom, yat kepyt yat contre
Fra Ingliſmen, with help off yair ſupple
Cetoun and Lyll into ye baſs yai baid;
For Sothroune folk ſo gret maſtryſs had maid, 640
Yat all ye ſouth was tayn into yar hand.
And Hew ye Hay was ſend into Ingland,
And oyir ayrs to preſoune at yair will.
To northland lordis faw no help cum yaim till,
A ſquier Guthre amang yaim ordand yai,   645
To

To warn Wallace in all ye haift he may.
Out off Arbroth he paffyt to ye fe.
And at ye flus fone takyn land had he;
In Flandrys land no refidens he maid,
In France he paft, bot Wallace weyll abaid 650
On hys purpofs in Gyan at ye wer,
On Sothroune men he had doyn mekill der.
Quhill gud Guthre had gottyn hys prefens,
He haiftyt hym, fone and maid no refidens;
He has hym tald, with Scotland how it ftud. 655
Yan Wallace faid, yi tithyngs ar nocht gud,
I had exampill off tym yat is by worn,
Trewys not to bynd with yaim yat was maynfuorn:
Bot I as yan couth nocht think on fic thing,
Becaufs yat we tuk yis pefs with yair King. 660
Be yair Chanflar ye toyir pefs was bun,
And yat full fair our forfadris has fun;
Undyr yat trew auctand fcor yai gert de,
At noblis war, ye beft in our cuntre.
To ye gret God my wow now her I mak, 665
Pefs with ye King I thing neuir for to tak,
He fall repent, yat yai yis wer began.
Yus mowit he, with mony ryoll man,
On to ye King, and tald hym hys entent.
Till lat hym pafs ye King wald nocht confent, 670
Quhill yar maid promyfs be hys hand,
Gyff euir agayn he thocht to leyff Scotland,
To cum till hym; hys gret feyll he hym gaiff
Off quhat Lordfchip yat he likyt to haiff.
Yus at ye King haifty leyff tuk he. 675

Na

Na ma with hym he brocht off yat cuntre,
Bot hys awin men, and Schyr Thomas ye Knycht.
In Flawndrys land yai paft with all yair mycht.
Guthreis barge was at ye flus left ftyll,
To fe yai went with a full egyr wyll.   680
Bath Forth and Tay yai left and paffit by
On ye north coft, Guthre was yair gy.
In Munrofs hawyn yai brocht hym to ye land,
Till trew Scotts it was a blyth tithand.
Schyr Jhon Ramfay, yat worthi was and wycht, 685
Fra Ochtyrhoufs ye way he chefyt rycht,
To meite Wallace with men off armes ftrang;
Off hys duellyng yai had thocht wondyr lang.
Ye trew Ruwan come als withoutyn baid,
In Barnan wode he had hys lugyng maid.   690
Barkla be yat to Wallace femblyt faft,
With thre hundreth to Ochtyr-houfs he paft.
Le letrir day off Auguft fell yis cace,
For ye refkew, yus ordanyt wycht Wallace,
Off Santt Jhonftoune yat Sothroune occupyit; 695
Faft towart Tay yai paffit and afpyit,
Out off ye toun, as Scottfmen till hym faid,
Or it was day undyr Kinnowll yaim laid,
Yat ferwandys oyfyt with carts hay to leid,
So was it futh, and hapnyt into deid;   700
Sax fum yar com, and brocht bot carts thre.
Quhen yai off hay was ladand moft byffe,
Guthre with ten in handys has yaim tayn,
Put yaim to dede, off yaim he fawyt nayn.
Wallace gart tak in haift yar himeft weid,   705
And

And fic lik men yai waillyt with gud fpeid;
Four war rycht rud, Wallace hymfelff tuk ane,
A ruffyt clok, and with hym gud Ruwane,
Guthrie, with yat and als gud zemen twa,
In yat ilk foit yai graithit yaim to ga.   710
Full futelly yai coueryt yaim with hay,
Syne to ye toun yai went ye gaynest way.
Fyfteyn yai tuk off men in armes wycht,
In ilk cart fyffe yai ordanyt out off fycht;
Yir cartars had fchort fuerds, off gud fteill,   715
Undyr yair weids, callyt furth ye carts weill.
Schyr Jhon Ramfay baid with a bufchement ftill
Quhen myftir war to help yaim with gud will.
Yir trew cartars paft withoutyn lett,
Atour ye bryg, and entryt throw ye zet;   720
Quhen yai war in, yair clokis keft yaim fra,
Gud Wallace yan ye mayftir portar can ta.
Apon he hed, quhill ded he has hym left,
Syne oyir twa ye lyff fra yaim has reft.
Guthrie, be yat, did rycht weill in ye toun,   725
And Ruwan als dang off yai famen doun.
Ye armyt men, was in ye carts brocht,
  Raifs up and weill yair dewory has wrocht;
Apon ye gait yai gert feill Sothroune de.
Ye Ramfais fpy has feyn get entre.   730
Ye bufchement brak, bath bryg and port has won,
Into ye toun gret ftryff yar was begon.
Yai twentye men, or Ramfay come in playn,
Within ye toun had fexty Sothroune flayn.
Ye Inglifmen on till aray was gayn,   735
                                            Ye

Ye Scotts as yan layfer lett yaim get nayn;
Fra gud Ramfay with hys men entryt in,
Yai fawit nayn was born off Inglis kyn.
Als Longaweill, ye wycht Knycht Schyr Thomas,
Prowyt weill yan and in, mony oyir place; 740
Agayn hys dynt few Inglifmen mycht ftand,
Wallace with hym gret faith and kyndnes fand.
Ye Sothroune part faw weill ye toun was tynt,
Frefchly yai ferd, as fyr dois out off flynt.
Sum fled, fum fell into draw dykis deip, 745
Sum to ye kyrk, yair lyffs giff yai mycht keip;
Sum fled to Tay, and in fmall wefchell zeid,
Sum derfly deit and drownyt in yat fteid.
Schyr Jhon Sewart at ye weft port outpaft,
Till Meffen wod he fped hym wondyr faft. 750
A hundreth men ye kyrk tuk for fuccour,
Bot Wallace wald no Grace grant in yat hour.
He flay bad all off cruell Sothroune keyn;
And faid yai had to Santt Jhonftoune enymyfs beyn.
Four hundreth men into ye toun war dede, 755
Sewyn fcor with lyff chapyt out off yat fted.
Wyffs and barnys yai maid yaim fre to ga,
With Wallace wyll he wall fla nayn off ya.
Ryches yai fand, yat Inglifmen had brocht new,
Syne plenyft ye toun with worthi Scotts trew. 760
Schyr Jhon Sewart left Meffen foreft ftrang,
Went to ye Gafk with feyll Sothroune amang;
And fyne in Fyff, qubar Wallang fcherriff was,
Send carrours fone out throuch ye land to pafs,
And gadryt men a ftalwart cumpany; 765

Till

Till Ardargan he drew yaim priwaly,
Ordand yaim in bargan reddy boun;
Agayn he thocht to failze Santt Jhonftoun,
Quhar Wallace lay, and wald na langar reft,
Rewllyt ye toun as yat hym lykit beft. 770
Schyr Jhon Ramfay gret Captane ordand he,
Ruwan fchirreff, at ane accord for to be.
Yis charge he gaiff, gyff men yaim warnyng maid.
To cum till hym withoutyn mor abaid;
And fo yai did, quhen tithings was yaim brocht. 775
With a hundreth Wallace furth fra yaim focht.
To Fyff he paft, to wefy yat cuntre,
Bot wrang warnyt off Inglifman was he.
Schyr Jhon Sewart, quhen yai war paffyt by,
Fra he Ochell he fped hym haiftely; 780
Upon Wallace folowit in all hys mycht,
In Abyrnethy tuk lugyng yat fyrft nycht.
Apon ye morn, with fyfeteyn hundreth men,
Till Blak Irnfyde hys gydys couth yaim ken;
Yar Wallace was, and mycht na meffage fend 785
Till Santt Jhoneftoune, till mak yis jornay kend;
For Inglifmen, yat full futtell has beyn,
Gart wachis walk, yat nayn mycht pafs betweyn.
Yan Wallace faid, yis mater payis nocht me.
He cald till hym ye fquier gud Guthre, 790
And befet als, yat knew full weill ye land,
And aft at yaim quhat deid was beft on hand,
Meffage to mak, our power for to get,
With Sothroune fone we fall be undirfet;
And wykkyt Scotts, yat knawis yis forreft beft, 795

Yai

Yai ar ye caufs yat we may haiff no reft;
I dred fer mar Wallang, yat is yair gyd,
Yan all ye laiff yat cummys on yat fyd.
Yan Guthre faid, mycht we get ane or tway,
To Santt Jhonftoune it war ye gayneft way, 800
And warn Ramfay, we wald get fuccour fone:
Ourfuth it is, it cannot now be don:
Rycht weyll I wait wefchell is lewyt nayn,
Fra ye Wode hawyn, to ye ferry cald Aran.
Yan Wallace faid, ye wattir cald it is, 805
Myfelff can fwym, I trow, and fall na myfs;
Bot currourfs oyfs yat gaynys nocht for me,
And I leyff zow her, zet had I leuir de:
Throw Godds Grace we fall bettir efchew,
Ye ftrenth is ftark, als we haiff men enew; 810
In Elchoch park, bot fourty yar war we,
For fewyn hundreth, and gert feill Sothroune de;
And chapyt weill in mony unlikly place,
So fall we her throw help off Goddis Grace:
Quhill men may faft, yir wodds we may hald ftill;
For yi, ilk man be off trew hardy will,
And at we do fo nobill into deid,
Off us be found no lak eftir to reid:
Ye rycht is ours, we fuld mor ardent be,
I think to freith yis land, or ellis de. 820
Hys waillyt fpech, with witt and hardyment,
Maid all ye layff fo cruell of entent,
Sum baid tak feild, and gyff battaill in playn.
Wallace faid, nay, yi wordis ar in wayn,
We will nocht leyff yat may be our wantage, 825

Ye

Ye wode till us is worth a zers wage.
Off hewyn temyr in haift he gert yaim tak,
Syllys off ayk, and a ftark barres mak,
At a foyr frount, faft in ye foreft fyd,
A full gret ftrenth, quhar yai purpoft to byd, 830
Stellyt yaim faft till treis yat growand was,
Yat yai mycht weyll in fra ye barres pafs,
And fo weill graithit, on ayir fyd about,
Syn com agayn, quhen yai faw yaim in dout.
Be yat ye ftrenth arayit was at rycht, 835
Ye Inglis oft approchit to yair fycht.
Yan Sewart com, yat way for till haiff wend,
As yai war wount, fa hys gydis yai kend.
At yat entre yai thocht to haiff paffage,
Bot fone yai fand yat maid yaim gret ftoppage. 840
A thoufand he led off men in armes ftrang,
With fyffe hundreth he gert Jhon Wallang gang
Without ye wode, yat nane fuld pafs yaim fra.
Wallace with hym had fourty archars thra,
Ye layff was fpers, full nobill in a ncid, 845
On yair enymyfs yai bykkyr with gud fpeid.
A cruell cuntyr was at ye barres feyn.
Ye Scotts Defens fo fekyr was and keyn,
Sothroune ftud aw to enter yaim amang;
Feill to ye ground yai ourthrew in yat thrang. 850
A rowm was left, quhar part in frount mycht fayr,
Quha entryt in, agayn zeid neuir mayr.
Fourty yai flew, yat formaft wald haiff paft.
All difarayit ye oft was, and agaft;
And part off horfs throw fchot to dede was brocht,

Brak to a playn, ye Sothroune fra yaim focht.
Ye Sewart faid, allace, how yis be,
And do no harm, our gret rabut haiff we;
He tald Wallang, and afkyt hys cunfaill,
Schyrreff yow art, quhat may be our awaill?   860
Bot few yai ar yat makis yis gret debait.
Jhon Wallang faid, yis is ye beft I wait,
To cefs hereoff, and remayn her befyd,
For yai may nocht lang in yis foreft byd
For fawt off fud, yai mon in ye contre;   865
Yan war mar tyme on yaim to mak melle:
Or yai be won be fors, into yis ftryff
Feill at ze leid fall erar lofs ye lyff.
Yan Sewart faid, yis reid I will nocht tak,
And Scotts be warnyt, refkew fone will yai mak; 870
Off yis difpyt amendys I think to haiff,
Or de yarfor in nowmyr with ye laiff;
In till a rang myfelff on fut will fayr.
Aucht hundreth he tuk off liklyaft yat was yar;
Syne bad ye layff bid at ye barres ftill   875
With Jhon Wallang, to rewll yaim at hys will.
Wallang, he faid, be forthwart in yis cace,
In fic a fwar we couth nocht get Wallace,
Tak hym or fla; I promefs ze be my lyff,
Yat King Edwarde fall mak yow Erle off Fyff;   880
At zon eft part we think to enter in,
I bid no mar, mycht ze yis barrefs wyn;
Fra yai be clofyt graithly amang us fa,
Bot merwill be yai fall na ferrar ga;
Affailze fayr, quhen ze witt we cum ner,   885
On

On ayir fyd we fall hald yaim on fter.
Yus femblyt yai apon ane awfull wyfs.
Wallace has feyn quhat was yair haill dewyfs.
Gud men, he faid, undirftud ze yis deid,
Forfuth yai ar rycht mekill for to dreid; 890
Zon Sewart is a nobill worthi Knycht,
Forthwart in wer, rycht worthi, wyfs and wycht;
Hys affailze he ordannys wondyr fayr
Us for to harm, no mannys wit can do mar;
Plefand it is to fe a Chyftayne ga 895
So Chyftanlik, it fuld recomfort ma
Till hys awn men, and yai off worfchip be,.
Yan for to fe ten thoufand cowarts fle:
Sen we ar ftad with euymyfs on ilk fyd,
And her on fors mon in yis foreft byd, 900
Yan fray ye fyrft, for Godds faik, cruellye.
Crawfurd he left, and Longaweill ye Knycht,
Fourty with yaim, to kepe ye barres wycht;.
With hym fexte off worthi men in weid,
To meit Sewart with hardy will yai zeid. 905
A maner dyk into yat wode was maid,
Off Thuortour ryfs, quhar bauldly yai abaid;
A downwart ye Sothroune to yaim had.
Sone femblyt yai with ftrakis far and fad:
Scharp fperys faft dufchand on ayir fyd, 910
Throw byrnys brycht maid woundys deip and wid.
Yis wantage was, ye Scotts yaim dantyt fwa,
Nayn Inglifmen durft fra hys feris ga,
To brek aray, or formaft entyr in.
Off Cryftin blud to fe it was gret fin, 915

For

For wrangwyfs caufs, and has beyn mony day.
Feyll Inglifmen in ye dyk deid yai lay.
Speris full fone all into fplyndrys fprang,
With fcharp fuerdys yai hew in yat thrang;
Blud byrftyt out throw fyn harnes off maill.   920
Jhon Wallang als full fcharply can affaill
Apon Crawfurd, and ye Knycht Longaweill,
At yar power kepyt ye barres weill,
Maid gud defens, be wyt, manheid and mycht,
At ye entre feill men to dede yai dycht.   925
Yus all at anys affailzeit in yat place,
Nayn yat was yar durft turn fra ye barrace
To help Wallace, nor nayn off hys durft pafs
To refkew yaim fo feyll ye fechtyng was;
At ayir ward handelyt yaim full hat,   930
Bot do or de na fuccour ellis yai wayt.
Wallace was ftad into yat ftalwart ftour,
Guthre, befat, with men off gret walour,
Rychard Wallace, yat worthi was off hand.
Sewart merwellyt, yat contrar yaim mycht ftand, 935
Yat euyr fa few mycht byd in battaill place,
Agaynys yaim, metyng face for face;
He thocht hymfelff to end yat mater weill,
Faft preffyt in with a gud fuerd off fteill,
Into ye dyk a Scottfman gert he de.   940
Wallace yaroff in hart had gret pyte;
Amendis till haiff he folowyt on hym faft,
But Inglifmen fa thik betwex yaim paft,
Yat apon hym a ftrak get mycht he nocht,
Oyir worthys derfly to dede he brocht.   945

Sloppys

Sloppys yai maid throw all ye chewalry,
Ye worthi Scotts yai wrocht fa worthely.
Yan Sothroune fa off yair gud men fad reft,
Langar to byd yai thocht it nocht ye beft.
Four fcor was flayn, or yai wald leiff yat fteid,   950
And fyftye als was at ye barrace deid.
A trumpet blew, and fra ye wode yai draw;
Wallang left off, yat fycht fra yat he faw.
To failze mar yaim thocht it was na fpeid,
Without ye wode to cunfaill fone yai zeid.   955
Ye worthi Scotts till reft yaim was full fayn,
Feill hurts had, bot few off yaim was flayn.
Wallace yaim bad off all gud comfort be,
Thankyt be God, ye fayrer part haiff we;
Zon Knycht Sewart has at gret jornay beyn,   960
Sa fair affay I haiff bot feildyn feyn,
I had leuir off Wallang wrokyn be,
Yan ony man yat is off zon menzhe.
Ye Scotts all on to ye barrefs zeid,
Stanchit wounds, yat couth full braithly bleid.   965
Part Scotts men had bled full mekill blud,
For fawt off drynk, and als wantyng off fud,
Sum feblyt faft yat had feill hurts yar.
Wallace yarfor fichit with hart full far.
A hat he bynt, to get wattir is gayn,   970
Oyir refut as yan he wyft off nayn;
A litill ftrand he fand, yat ryn hym by,
Off cler wattir, he brocht haboundandly,
And drank hymfelff, fyn faid, with fobyr mud,
Ye wyn off France me thocht not half fo gud.   975

Yan off ye day thre quartars was went.
Schyr Jhon Sewart has caftyn in hys entent,
To failze mar as yan he couth nocht preiff,
Quhill on ye morn yat mar men couth raleiff,
And kep yaim in, quhill yai, for hungyr for,   980
Cum in hys will, or ellis de yarfor.
Wallang, he faid, I charge you for to byd,
And kep yaim in, I will to Coupar ryd;
You fall remayn, with fyffe hundreth at yi will,
And I ye morn fall com with power ye till.   985
Jhon Wallang faid, yis charge I forfaik,
Eftir yis day all nycht I may nocht waik;
For, traits weyll, yai will ifche to ye playn,
Yocht ze byd, or ellis de in ye payn.
Sewart bad hym byd, undyr ye blaym,   990
I ye cummaund on gud King Edwards naym.
Or yar to God a wow I mak beforn,
And yai brek out, to hyng yow heych to morn.
Off yat cummaund Jhon Wallang had gret dreid;
Sewart went fra yaim with nyne fcor into deid   995
Next hand ye wode, and hys gud men off Fyff,
Yat with hym baid in all term off yair lyff.
Wallace drew ner, hys tyme quhen yat he faw,
To ye wode fyd, and couth on Wallang caw,
Zon Knycht to morn, has hecht to hyng ye hie,   1000
Cum in till us, I fall yi warrand be,
In contrar hym, and all King Edwards mycht,
Tak we hym quyk, I fall hym hyng on hycht;
And gud Lordfchip I fall gyff yow hereft
In yis ilk land, yat yi brodyr has left.   1005
Wallang

Wallang was wyfs, full fone can underftand,
Be lyklynes Wallace fuld wyn ye land,
And bettir hym war into ye rycht to byd,
Yan be in wer apon ye Sothroune fyd.
With fchort wyfment to Wallace in yai focht. 1010
Yan Sewart cryt, and faid, yat beis for nocht,
And fals off kynd yow art in heretage,
Edwarde on ye has waryt ewill gret wage;
Her I fall byd, my purpofs to fulfill,
Oyir to de, or haiff ye at my will. 1015
For all hys fpech to pafs he wald nocht fpar;
With full glaid hart Wallace refawit yaim yar.
Be yat, Ruwan and Ramfay off renoun,
Be a trew Scott, yat paft to Santt Jhonftoun,
Yaim warnyng maid, yat Sewart folowit faft 1020
Apon Wallace yan war yai far agaft;
Out off ye toun yai ufchyt with all yair mycht,
With thre hundreth, yat worthi war and wycht;
To Blak Irnfide affemblyt in yat place,
As Wallang was gane into gud Wallace. 1025
Ye Knycht Sewart has weill yair cummyng feyn,
A fayr playn feild he chefyt yaim betweyn.
Elewyn hundreth and four fcor yan had he;
Ye Scottfmen war fex hundreth and fexte.
Yai war bot few, a playn feild for to tak. 1030
Out off ye wode gud Wallace can yaim mak;
He wyft nathing off yaim yat cummyng was,
Mar hardyment was fra ye ftrenth to pafs:
Bot quhan yai hard Ruwan and Ramfay cry,
Off Ochtyrhoufs blyth was yat chewalry; 1035

Mycht

Mycht yai off gold haiff brocht a kings rent,
To gud Wallace mycht nocht fo weill content.
Yan till aray yai zeid on ayir fyd,
In cruell ire, in battaill bown to byd.
Worthear men yan Sewart femblyt yar, 1040
In all hys tym, Edwarde had neuir mar.
Bot Sewart faw hys nowmyr was fer ma,
Hys power fone he gert dewyd in twa;
To fecht at anys, rycht Knycht lik he yaim kend,
In yat jornay oyir to wyn or end. 1045
Ye worthi Scotts rufchyt on yaim in gret ire,
With cruell ftrakis, yat flamyt fers as fyr.
Wallace and hys, als Sothroune yat was yar,
Fell fpers hid, for feyll fechtand and far
Into ye wode at failze all ye day: 1050
Bot new cummyn men weill waillit fpers had yai;
Into ye ftour yai gert feill Sothroune de,
Yair cruell deid gret marwell was to fe.
Yai worthi Scotts, yat fyrft amang yaim baid,
Full gret flauchtir on Inglifmen yai maid; 1055
Into ye wode befor had prowit weyll,
Yan on ye playn yai fenzeit nocht adeill;
In curage grew, as yai war new begon,
Schort reft yai had fra ryffyng off ye fon.
Be yat gud Ramfay, and with hym gud Ruwan, 1060
Throuchout ye thikkeft off ye prefs is gan;
Sloppis yai maid throw out ye Inglifmen,
Diffeuyryt yaim be twenty and by ten.
Quhen fpers war gayn, with fuerdis off metall cler,
Till Inglifmen yar cummyng was fauld full der. 1065

Wallace

Wallace and hys, be worthines off hand,
Feyll Sothroune blud gart lye apon ye land.
Ye twa feildys togyddyr relyt yan
Schyr Jhon Sewart, with mony nobill man.
To help yair lord, with thre hundreth in place 1070
About hym ftud, and did yair befines,
Defendand hym, with mony awfull dynt,
Quhill all ye owtwart off ye feild was tynt.
Off comowns part into ye foreft fled
Succour to fek, yair men had yaim fa led. 1075
Ye Scotts has feyn fo mony in a rout
With Sewart ftand, na warrand yaim about,
Apon all fyd affailziet wondyr fayr;
Throw polyt platts with poynts perfyt yair.
Ye Sothroune made defens full cruelly, 1080
All occupyit was yis gud chewalry.
Schyr Jhon Ramfay wald yai had zoldyn beyn.
Wallace faid, nay, it is all wrang ye meyn,
Ranfoun to mak we can nocht now begyn,
On fic awyfs yis land we may not wyn 1085
Zon knycht off lang our ald enemy has beyn,
Sa fell till us off yaim I haiff nocht feyn:
Now he fall de, with help off Goddis Grace,
He com to pay hys ranfoun in yis place.
Ye Sothroune wyft all playnly for to de, 1090
Refkew was nayn, fuppos at yai wald fle,
Frefchlye yai faucht as yai entryt new,
Apon our fyd part worthi men yai flew.
Yan Sewart faid, allace, throw wrangwis thing 1095
Our lywys we lofs, throw defyr off our King.

Ye felloune Knycht dowted hys dede rycht nocht,
Amang ye Scotts full manfully he wrocht,
Befat he ftraik to dede withoutyn mar.
Wallace preft in, with hys fuerd burnyft bar,
At Sewart als he etlyt in gret ire, 1100
Throw peffanis ftuff in fondyr ftrak ye fwyr;
Dede to ye ground he dufchyt for all hys mycht,
Off Wallace hand yus endyt yus gud Knycht.
Ye ramaynand without mercy yai fla,
For gud befat ye Scotts war wondyr wa. 1105
In handis fum yai ftraik without remeid,
Na Sothroune paft with lyff out off yat fted.
Yan to ye wode, for yaim yat left ye feild,
A rang fet, yus yai may get na beild.
Zeid nayn away was contrar our punzoun. 1110
Gud Ruwan paft agayn to Santt Jhonftoun.
Schyr Jhone Ramfay to Cowper Caftill raid,
Yat houfs he tuk, for defens nane was maid.
Wallace Crawfurd, and with yaim gud Guthrie,
Rychard Wallace had lang beyn in melle, 1115
And Longaweill into Lundors baid ftill,
Faftyt yai had to lang agayn yair will.
Wallang yai maid yair ftwart for to be,
Off meit and drink yai fand aboundanle.
Ye priour fled, and durft na reknyng byd, 1120
He was befor apon ye toyir fyd.
Apon ye morn to Santt Androwis yai paft,
Out off ye toun yat byfchop turnyt faft.
Ye King off Ingland had hym yiddyr fend,
Ye rent at will he gaiff hym in commend, 1125

Hys

Hys Kings charge as yan he durſt nocht hald,
A wrangwys Pape yat tyrand mycht be cald;
Few fled with hym, and gat away be ſe,
For all Scotland he wald nocht Wallace ſe.
As yan off hym he maid bot lycht record,   1130
Gert reſtor hym yat yar was rychtwyſs lord.
Ye worthi Knycht, yat into Coupar lay,
Gart ſpulze it apon ye ſecund day;
Syne ordand men, at ye cummaund off Wallace,
Bot mar proceſs, for to caſt doun yat place.   1135
Mynours ſone yai gert preſs throw ye wall,
Syne pounceounis fyryt, and to ye ground keſt all.
Schyr Jhon Ramſay ſyne to ye kyrk can fayr,
Sothroune was fled, and left but wallis bayr;
Eftir Sewart yai durſt nocht tary lang.   1140
Ye Scotts at large throw all Fyff yai rang.
Off Ingliſmen nayn left in yat cuntre,
Bot in Lochlewyn yar lay a cumpane,
Apon yat Inch, in a ſmall houſs yai dycht,
Caſtell was nayn, bot wallyt with wattir wycht. 1145
Beſyd carraill yai ſemblyt Wallace beforn,
Hys purpoſs was for till aſſay Kyngorn.
A Knycht hecht Gray yan Captane in it was,
Be ſchort awyſs purpos he tuk to pas,
Erar he wald byd chalans off hys King,   1150
Yan with Wallace to rakyn for ſic a thing.
Yat houſs yai tuk, and littill tary maid.
Apon ye morn, withoutyn mair abaid,
Atour ye mur, quhar yai a tryſt had ſet,
Ner Scotlands well yair lugyng tuk bot let.   1155

Eftir

Eftir foupar Wallace baid yaim ga reft,
Myfelff will walk, me think it may be beft.
As he cummandyt, but grathing yai haiff don.
Into yair flep Wallace hym graithit fon,
Paft to Lochlewyn as it was ner mydnycht,   1160
Auchtand with hym, yat he had warnyt rycht;
Yir men wend weill he com to wefy it.
Falows, he faid, I do yow weill to wyt,
Confidyr weill yis place, and undirftand,
Yat it may do full gret fcaith to Scotland,   1165
Out off ye fouth and power com yaim till,
Yai may tak in, and kepe it at yair awne will;
Apon zon Inch rycht mony mar may be,
And fyne ufche out, yair tym quhen at yai fe.
To byd lang her we may nocht apon chans,   1170
Zon folk has fud, traift weyll, at fufficians;
Wattir fra yaim forfuth can nocht be fet,
Sum oyir wyill us worthis for to get;
Zhe fall remayn her at yis port all ftill,
And I myfelff ye boit fall bryng yow till.   1175
Yarwith in haift hys weid off cafts he,
Apon zon fyd na wachman can I fe,
Held on hys fark, and tuk hys fuerd fo gud
Band on hys nek, and fyne lap in ye flud,
And our he fwam, for lattyng fand he nocht.   1180
Ye boit he tuk, and till hys men it brocht;
Arayit hym weill, and wald na langar byd,
Bot paffit in, rowit to ye toyir fyd.
Ye Inch yai tuk with fuerds drawyn in hand,
And fparyt nayn yat yai befor yaim fand,   1185

Strak

Strak durs up, ſtekyt quhar yai lay,
Apon ye Sothroune yus ſadly ſemblyt yai.
Threty yai flew, yat was in yat ſamyn place,
To mak defens ye Ingliſmen had no ſpace.
Yair wemen fyffe Wallace ſend off yat ſtede,   1190
Woman nor barn he gert neuir put to dede.
Ye gud yai tuk, as it had beyn yair awyn,
Yan Wallace ſaid, fallowis, I mak zow knawyn,
Ye purwyance, yat is within yis wanys,
We will nocht tyne, gert ſembyll all at anys,   1195
Gar warn Ramſay, and our gud men ilk an,
I will remayn quhill yis warn ſtor began;
Send furth a man yair horſs for to keip,
Drew up ye boit, ſyne beddys tuk to ſleip.
Wallace power, quhilk Scotland well ner lay,   1200
Befor ye ſon yai myſſyt hym away.
Sum menyng maid, and merwellyt off yat cace.
Ramſay bad ceſs, and murn nocht for Wallace,
It is for gud yat he is fra us went,
It ſall ze ſe, traiſt weill, in werrament;   1205
My hed to wed Lochlewyn he paſt to ſe,
Bot yat is yar no Ingliſmen knaw we,
In all yis land, betwix yir wattris left,
Tithands off hym ze ſall ſe ſon hereft.
As yai about was talkand on yis wyſs,   1210
A meſſage com, and chargyt yaim to ryſs.
My Lord, he ſaid, to dyner has zow cald
Into Lochlewyn, quhilk is a ryoll hald,
Ze ſall fayr weyll, yarfor put off all ſorow.
Yai graithit yaim rycht ayrly on ye morow,   1215

And yidder paft, off Wallace will to wytt;
Yus femblyt yai in a full blyth falowfchip.
Yai lugyt yar till aucht dayis was at end,
Off meit and drynk yai had inewch to fpend;
Turffyt furth ger, yat Sothroune had brocht yar 1220
Gert byrn ye boit, till Santt Jhonftoune yai fair.
Byfchope Synclar, yat worthi was and wyfs,
Till Wallace com, and tauld hym hys awyfs;
Yus he defyryt Wallace fuld with hym ryd,
And in Dunkell foiourn yat wyntyr tyd. 1225
Bot he faid, nay, yat hald I nocht ye beft,
And Scotland yus, in pefs we can nocht reft.
Ye Byfchop faid, playnly ze may nocht wend,
Into ye north for men I red zow fend.
I grant, quoth he, and cheiffit a meffynger. 1230
Ye worthi Jop was with ye Byfchop yar,
And mayftir Blair Wallace com bot baid,
With yat gud Lord yat nobill cher yaim maid.
Wallace fend Blair, in hys preifts weid,
To warn ye weft, quhar freyndys had gret dreid 1235
How yai fuld pafs, or to gud Wallace wyn,
For Inglifmen, yai held yaim lang in twyn.
Adam Wallace, and Lindfay yat was wycht,
Rawchle yai left, and left away be nycht,
Throw out ye land to ye Lennox yai cayr, 1240
Till Erle Malcom, yat welcumyt yaim full fayr.
Maifter Jhon Blair was blyth off yat femble,
Gud Grayme was yar, and Richard off Lunde,
Als Robert Boid, yat out off But yaim focht;
Had yai Wallace off no thing ellis yai rocht; 1245

Bot

Bot Inglifmen betwix yaim was fa ftrang,
Yat yai in playn mycht not weill to hym gang.
Jop paft north, for leiching wald nocht let,
Gret power yar as yan he couth nocht get;
Ye Lord Cumyng, yat Erle off Bouchane was, 1250
For auld Inwy he wald na man pafs
Yat he mycht let, in gud Wallace fupple,
For Erle Patrik a playn feild kepyt he.
Zet pur men com, and prowyt all yair mycht
To help Wallace, in fens off Scotlands rycht. 1255
Ye gud Randell in tendyr age was kend,
Part off men out off Murray he did fend.
Jop paft agayn, and com in prefens fone
Befor Wallace, and tald quhow he had don;
Bot Mayftyr Blair fa gud tithyngs hym brocht, 1260
Yat off Cumyng Wallace full litill roucht
Als Inglifmen had yan full littill dreid,
Fra Fyff was tynt ye war yai trowit to fped.
Ye Duk and Erle, yat in Scotland yaim led,
Captanys yai maid, in Ingland fyn yaim fped. 1265
Wallace hym bownyt, quhen he thocht tym fuld be,
Off Santt Jhonftoune, and with hym tuk fyfte.
Stewyn off Irland, and Kerle yat was wycht,
For Inglifmen yai had haldyn ye hycht
In wachman lyff, and fendyt yaim rycht weyll, 1270
Till gud Wallace yai war as trew as fteyll,
To folow hym ye twa thocht neuyr lang.
Throw out ye Ochell yai maid yaim for to gang,
Off mar power he taryt nocht yat tyd,
To keip ye land he gert ye layff abyd; 1275

To Styrlyng Bryg as yan he wald not pafs,
For ftrang power off Inglifmen yar was.
Till Erth ferry yai paffit prewaly,
And bufchit yaim in a dern fted yarby.
A cruell Captayne in Erth dueit yar,   1280
In Ingland born, and hecht Thomylyn off Wayr.
A hundreth men was at hys ledyng ftill,
To bruk yat land yai did power and will.
A Scotts fyfchar, quhilk yai had tayn beforn,
Contrar hys will gert hym be to yaim fuorn,   1285
In ye feruice yai held hym day and nycht.
Befor ye fon Wallace gert Jop hym dycht,
And fend hym forth ye paffage for to fpy;
On yat fyfchar he hapnyt fodandly,
All hym allayn, bot a boy yat was yar;   1290
Jop hynt hym fone, and for na dreid wald fpar,
Be ye collar, and out a knyff hynt he.
For Godds faik yis man afkyt merce.
Jop fperyt fone, off quhat natioun art yow?
A Scott, he faid, bot Sothroune gart me bow   1295
In yair feruice, agayn my will full fayr,
Bot for my lyff yat I ramaynyt yair;
To fek fyfche I com on yis north fyd,
Be ze a Scott, I wald fayn with yow byd.
Yan he hym brocht in prefens to Wallace.   1300
Ye Scotts was blyth quhen yai haiff feyn yis cace,
For with hys bait yai mycht weill paffage haive;
For fery craft na fraucht he thocht to craive.
Apon yat fyd langar yai taryed nocht,
Till ye fouth land with glaid harts yai focht; 1305
                                            Syne

Syne brak ye bait, quhen yai war landyt yair,
Seruice off it Sothroune mycht haiff na mayr.
Yan throuch ye mofs yai paffit full gud fpeid
Till ye Torwode, yis man with yaim yai leid.
Ye wedow yar brocht tithands to Wallace,   1310
Off hys trew Eyme yat duelt at Dunypace,
Thomlyn off Wayr in prefoun had hym fet,
For mar trefour na he befor mycht get.
Wallace faid, deym, he fall weill lowfyt be,
Be none to morn, or ma yarfor fall de.   1315
Sche gat yaim meit, and in quiet yai baid
Quhill yai was rycht, fyne redy fone yaim maid,
Towart Arthall rycht fodeynly yaim drew.
A ftrenth yar was, yat weyll ye fyfchar knew,
Off draw dykis, and full off wattir wan,   1320
Wyfly yaroff has warnyt yaim yis man.
On ye bak fyd he led yaim prewale,
Fra ye wattir as wont to cum was he,
Our a fmall bryg. Gud Wallace entryt in
Into ye hall, hymfelff thocht to begyn;   1325
Fra ye fowper as yai war bown to ryfs,
He faluft yaim apon ane awfull wyfs;
Hys men hym folowit fodanly at anys,
Haifty forow was raffyt in yai wanys;
With fcherand fuerds fcharply about yaim dang,   1330
Feill on ye flur was fellyt yaim amang.
With Thomlyn Wayr Wallace hymfelff has met,
A felloune ftraik fadly apon hym fet,
Throch hede and fwyr all throuch ye coft hym claiff;
Ye worthy Scotts faft ftekyt off ye laiff,   1335

Kepyt durs, and dulfully yaim dycht,
To chaip away ye Sothroune had no mycht.
Sum wyndowys focht for till haiff brokyn out,
Bot all for nocht, full fey was maid yat rout.
About ye fyr brufchyt ye blud fo red,   1340
A hundreth men was flayn into yat fted.
Yan Wallace focht quhar hys uncle fuld be;
In a dyrk cawe he was fet dulfulle,
Quhar wattir ftud, and he in yrnyfs ftrang.
Wallace full fone ye braffis up he dang;   1345
Off yat myrk holl brocht hym with ftrenth and lyft,
Bot noyis he hard, off no thing ellis he wyft;
So blyth befor in warld he had nocht beyn,
As yar, with fycht quhen he had Wallace feyn.
In dykys owt ye dede bodyis yai keft,   1350
Graithyt ye place as at yaim lykyt beft,
Maid ftill gud cher, and wyfs wachis gert fet,
Quhill ner ye day yai flepe withoutyn let;
Quhen yai had lycht fpulziet ye place in hy,
Fand gayn and ger, bathe gold and jowelry;   1355
Our all yat day in quiet held yai ftill;
Quhat Sothroune come, yai refawit with gud will,
In yat laubour ye Scotts was full vayn,
Inglifmen com, bot nayn zeid owt agayn.
Women and barnys put in prifouns caive,   1360
So yai mycht mak no warnyng to ye laive;
Stewyn off Irland, and Kerle, yat war hycht,
Kepyt ye port apon ye fecund nycht.
Befor ye day ye worthi Scotts rayfs,
Turffit gud ger, and to ye Torwod gayfs,   1365

                      Remaynyt

Remaynyt yar quhill nycht was cummyn on hand,
Syne bownyt yaim in quiet throuch ye land.
Ye wedowis fone, fra yai had paffit dout,
A ferwand fend, and leit ye wemen out,
To pafs fra Arth, quhar at yaim lykyt beft.   1370
Now fpek off yaim yat went into ye weft.
Wallace hymfelff was fekyr gyd yat nycht,
Till Dunbertane ye way he chefyt rycht,
Or it was day, for yan ye nycht was lang,
On to ye toun full priwaly yai gang;   1375
Mekill off it Inglifmen occapyit.
Gud Wallace fone throw a dyrk gyrth hym hyit,
And till a houfs, quhar he was wont to ken,
A wedow duelt was fred full till our men;
Abowne hyr bed, on ye bakfyd, was maid   1380
A dern wyndow, was noyir lang nor braid,
Yar Wallace cauld, and fone fra fche hym knew,
In haift fche raifs, and prewaly yaim in drew
Till a clofs bern, quhar yai mycht kepyt be;
Baith meit and drynk fche brocht in gret plenté.   1385
A gudly gyft to Wallace als fche gaiff,
A hundreth pound, and mar, atour ye laiff.
Nyne fonnys fche had was lykly men and wycht,
Ane ayth till hym fche gart yaim fuer full rycht;
In pefs yai duelt, in trubyll yat had beyn,   1390
And trewbuit payit till Inglis Captaynes keyn.
Schir Jhon Menteth ye caftell had in hand,
Bot fum men faid, yat was a priwa band
To Sothroune maid, be menys off yat Knycht,
In yar fupple to be in all hys mycht;   1395
Yaroff

Yaroff as now I will na procefs mak.
Wallace yat day a fchort purpofs can tak;
Quhen it was nycht he bad ye wedow pafs,
Merk all ye durs quhar Sothroune duelland was;
Syne eftir yis he and hys chewalry   1400
Graithit yaim weill, and wappynys tuk on hy,
Went on ye gayt, quhen Sotheroune was on flep.
A gret oyftre our Scotts tuk to kep.
Ane Inglis Captane was fittand up fo lait,
Quhill he and hys with drynk was maid full mait. 1405
Nyne men was yar, now fet in hie curage,
Sum wald haiff had gud Wallace in yat rage,
Sum wald haiff bound Schyr Jhone ye Grame throuch
    ftrenth,
Sum wald haiff had Boid at ye fuerds lenth,
Sum wyft Lundy, yat chapyt was Fyff,   1410
Sum wychter was na Cetoun into ftryff,
Quhen Wallace hard ye Sothroune mak fic dyn,
He gart all byd, and hym allayn went in;
Ye layff remaynyt to her off yir tithans.
He faluft yaim with fturdy contenans.   1415
Falowis, he faid, fen I com laft fra haym,
In trawaill I was our land and uncouth fame,
Fra fouth Ireland I com in yis cuntre,
Ye conqueft off Scotland for to fe;
Part off your drynk, or fum gud I wald haiff. 1420
Ye Captayne a fchrewd anfuer hym gaiff,
Yow femys a Scott, unlikly us to fpy,
Yow may be ane off Wallace cumpany;
Contrar our King he is ryffyn agane,
                      Ye

Ye land off Fyff he has rademyt in plane; 1425
Zow fall her byd quhill we wyt quhow it be,
Be yow off hys, zow fall be hyngyt hye.
Wallace yan thocht it was na tyme to ftand,
Hys nobill fuerd he gryppyt fone in hand,
Awkwart ye face drew yat Captane in teyn, 1430
Straik all away yat ftud abowne hys cyn;
Ane oyir braithly in ye breyft he bar,
Baith brawn and bayn ye burly blaid throch fchar.
Ye layff rufchyt up to Wallace in gret ire,
Ye thryd he feld full ferfly in ye fyr. 1435
Stewyn off Irland, and Kerle, in yat thrang,
Kepyt na charge, bot entryt yaim amang,
And oyir ma yat to ye dur can prefs,
Quhill yai hym faw yar coud na thing yaim cefs.
Ye Sothroune men full fone was brocht to ded. 1440
Ye blyth Hoftelar bad yaim gud ayle and breid.
Wallace faid, nay, till we haiff layfar mar,
To be our gyd yow fall befor us fayr,
And begyn fyr quhar at ye Sothroune lyis.
Ye Hoftelar fone, apon a hafty wyfs, 1445
Hynt fyr in hand, and till a gret houfs zeid,
Quhar Inglifmen war in full mekill dreid;
For yai wyft nocht quhill yat ye rud low raifs,
As wood befts amang ye fyr yaim gaes,
With panyis fell rufchyt full forowfully. 1450
Ye layff without off our gud chewalry,
At ilka houfs, quhar ye Hoftillar began,
Kepyt ye durs, fra yaim chapyt na man,
For all yair mycht, yocht King Edwarde had fuorn,

Gate

Gate nayn away yat was off Ingland born, 1455
Bot oyir brynt, or but refkew was flayn,
And fum throuch fors drywyn in ye fyr agayn.
Part Scotts folk in feruice yaim amang,
Fra ony payn frely yai leit yaim gang.
Thre hundreth men was to Dimbertan fend, 1460
To kep ye land, as yair lords yaim kend,
Skaithlefs off yaim for ay was yis regioun.
Wallace or day maid hym out off ye toun,
On to ye Coyff off Dimbartane yai zeid,
And all yat day foiornyt out off dreid, 1465
Bathe meit and drynk ye Hoftillar gert be brocht.
Quhen nycht was cummyn, in all ye haift yai mocht,
Towart Roffneth full erneftfully yai gang,
For Inglifmen was in yat caftell ftrang.
On ye Garlouth yai purpoft yaim to bid, 1470
Betwix ye kyrk, yat ner was yar befyd,
And to ye caftell full priwaly yai draw,
Undyr a bray yai bufchyt yaim rycht law,
Lang ye wattir, quhar comoun oyfs had yai,
Ye caftellis ftuff on to ye kyrk ilk day. 1475
A mariage als yat day was to begyn,
All ufchyt owt, and left nayn within.
At fens mycht mak, bot fcherwandis in yat place;
Yus to yat tryft yai paffit upon cace.
Wallace and hys drew yaim full priwaly 1480
Ner hand ye place; quhen yai war paffit by,
Within ye hauld, and thocht to kep yat fteid
Fra Sothroune men, or ellis yarfor be deid.
Compleit was maid ye mariage into playn,

On to Roſſneth ȝai raturnyt agayn;   1485
Four ſcor and ma was in ȝat cumpany,
Bot nocht arayit as was our chewalry;
To ye caſtell ȝai weynd to paſs, but let.
Ye worthy Scotts ſa hardly on ȝaim ſet,
Fourtye at anys derfly to ground ȝai bar;   1490
Ye ramaynand affrayit was ſa far,
Langar in feild ȝai had no mycht to byd,
Bot ferſly fled fra ȝaim on ayir ſyd.
Ye Scotts ȝar has weill ye entre woun,
And ſlew ye laiff ȝat in ȝat houſs was foun;   1495
Syne on ye flears folowed wondyr faſt,
Na Ingliſman ȝar fra ȝaim with lyff at paſt.
Ye wemen ſone ȝai ſeſyt into hand,
Kepyt ȝaim cloſs, for warnyng off ye land.
Ye dede bodyis all out off ſycht ȝai keſt,   1500
Yan at gud eſs ȝai maid ȝaim for to reſt;
Off purweance ſewyn dayis ȝai lugit ȝar
At rud coſts, to ſpend ȝai wald nocht ſpar;
Quhat Sothroune com, ȝai tuk all glaidly in,
Bot owt agayn ȝai leit nane off ȝat kyn;   1505
Quha tithands ſend to ye Captayne off ȝat ſteid,
Yair ſcherwitours ye Scotts put to ded,
Spulziet ye place, and left na gud ȝar,
Brak wallis doun, and maid ȝat byggyng bar.
Quhen ȝai had ſpilt off ſtayne werk at ȝai mocht,
Syne kendyllit fyr, and fra Roſneth ȝai ſocht.
Quhen ȝai had brynt all tre-work in ȝat place,
Wallace gert freith ye wemen, off hys grace,
To do ȝaim harm neuir hys purpoſs was.

Yan

Yan to Faflan ye worthi Scotts can pafs, 1515
Quhar Erle Malcom was bydand at defence,
Rycht glaid he was off Wallace gud prefence;
Yan he fand yar a nobill cumpany,
Schyr Jhon ye Grame, and Richard off Lundy,
Adam Wallace, yat worthi was and wyfs, 1520
Berkla and Boid, with men mekill to pryfs.
At Criftenmefs yar Wallace foiornyt ftill;
Off hys modyr tithands war brocht hym till,
Yat tym befor fche had left Elriſle,
For Inglifmen in it fche durft nocht be; 1525
Fra ynce dyfgyfyt fche paft in pilgrame weid,
Sum gyrth to fek to Dunfermlyn fche zeid;
Seknes hyr had fo focht into yat fted,
Deceft fche was, God tuk hyr fpreit to leid.
Quhen Wallace hard at yat tithands war trew, 1530
Low fadnefs fo in ilka fid can perfew;
In thank he tuk, becaufs it was naturaill,
He lowyt God with fekyr hart and haill;
Bettyr hym thocht, yat it was hapnyt fa,
Na Sothroune fuld hyr put till oyir wa. 1535
He ordand Jop, and als ye mayftir Blayr,
Yiddyr to pafs, and for no cofts fpayr,
Bot honour do ye corp till fepulcur.
At hys commaund yai fcheruit ilka hour,
Doand yarto as dede afkis till haive, 1540
With worfchip wax ye corp graithit in graive.
Agayn yai turnyt, and fchawit hym off hyr end.
He thankyt God quhat Grace yat euir he fend;
He feis ye warld fa full off fantafie,

Confort

Confort he tuk, and leit all murnyng be; 1545
Hys maift defyr was for to freith Scotland.
Now will I tell quhat new cafs com on hand.
Schyr Wilzham lang off Douglacedaill was Lord;
Off hys fyrft wyff, as rycht was to record,
Deceft or yan, out off yis warldly cayr, 1550
Twa fonnys he had with hyr, yat leyffat yar,
Quhilk likly war, and abill in curage,
To fculle was fend into yair tendre age;
Jamys and Hew, fo hycht yir brethyr twa,
And eftir fone yair uncle couth yaim ta, 1555
Gud Robert Keth had yaim fra Glafkow toun,
Atour ye fe in France he maid yaim boun;
At ftudy fyne he left yaim into Parys,
With a maiftyr yat worthi was and wyfs.
Ye King Edwarde tuk yair fadyr ye Knycht, 1560
And held hym yar, yocht he was neuir fo wycht,
Till hym he had affentyt till hys will;
A mariage als yai gert ordand yaim till,
Ye Lady ferfs, off power and hie blud,
Bot yaroff com till hys lyff litill gud. 1565
Twa fonnys he gat on yis Lady but mar.
With Edwardes will he tuk hys leyff to far.
In Scotland com, and broucht hys wyff on pefs,
In Dowglas duelt, forfuth yis is no lefs.
King Edwarde trowit yat he had ftedfaft beyn, 1570
Faft to yair faith; bot ye contrar was feyn,
Ay Scotts blud remaynyt into Douglace,
Agayn Ingland he prowyt in mony place.
Ye Sawchar was a Caftell fayr and ftrang,

Ane Inglis Captayne, yat dyd feyll Scotts wrang,
Intill it duelt, and Bewffurd he was cauld,
Yat held all wayſt fra ynce to Douglace hald,
Rycht ner off kyn was Douglace wyff and he,
Yarfor he trowit in peſs off hym to be.
Schyr Wilȝam ſaw at Wallace raiſs agayn,   1580
And rycht likly to freith Scotland off payn;
Till help hym part intill hys mind he keſt,
For in yat lyff rycht lang he coud nocht leſt;
He thocht na charge to brek upon Ingland,
It was throuch force yat euir he maid yaim band.
A ȝong man yan, yat hardy was and bauld,
Born to hymſelff, and Thom Dycſon was cauld,
Der freynd, he ſaid, I wald preiff at my mycht,
And mak a fray to fals Bewfurd ye Knycht,
In Sawchar duellys, and dois full gret outrage. 1590
Yan Dycſon ſaid, myſelff in yat wiage
Sall with yow paſs, with Anderſon to ſpek,
Cuſyng to me, freyndſchip he will nocht brek;
For yat ilk man yair wode ledys yaim till,
Throch help off hym purpoſs ȝe may fulfill.   1595
Schyr Wilȝham yan, in all ye haiſt he mycht,
Threty trew men in yis wiage he dycht;
And tauld hys wyff till Dumfreſs he wald fayr,
A tryſt, he ſaid, off Ingland he had yair.
Yus paſſyt he quhar yat na Sothroune wyſt,   1600
With yir threty throw waiſt land at hys lyſt;
Quhill nycht was cummyn he buſchit yaim full law
In a clewch ner till ye wattyr off Craw.
To ye Sawchar Dycſon allayn he ſend,

             And

And he fone maid with Anderfon yis end, 1605
Dicfon fuld tak bathe hys horfs and hys weid,
Be it was day, a drawcht off wode to leid.
Agayn he paft, and tauld ye gud Douglace,
Quhilk drew hym fone intill a priway place.
Anderfon tauld quhat ftuff yat was yarin 1610
Till Jhon Dycfon, yat was ner off hys kyn,
Fourty yai ar off men off mekill waill,
Be yai on fute yai will zow far affaill;
Gyff yow hapnys ye entre for to get,
On yi rycht hand a ftalwart ax is fet, 1615
Yarwith zow may defend ze in a thrang,
Be Douglace wyfs he byds nocht fra yow lang.
Anderfon zeid to ye bufchement in hy,
Ner ye caftell he drew yaim priwaly
Intill a fchaw, (Sothroune myftrayftit nocht) 1620
To ye next wode, with Dycfon, fyn he focht,
Graithit hym a draucht, on a breid flip and law,
Changyt a horfs, and to ye houfs can caw;
Arayit he was in Anderfonnis weid,
And bad hym haiff in. Ye portar com gud fpeid,
Yis hour, he faid, yow mycht haive been away,
Untymys you art, for it is fcantly day.
Ye zet zeid up, Dicfon gat in but mar,
A thourtour baude, yat all ye drawcht up bar,
He cuttyt it, to ground ye flyp can ga, 1630
Cumryt ze zet, ftekyng yai mycht not ma;
Ye portar fone he hynt into yat ftryff,
Twyfs throuch ye hede he ftekyt hym with a knyff.
Ye ax he gat, yat Anderfon off fpak,

A bekyn maid, yarwith ye bufchment brak.   1635
Douglace hymfelff was formaſt in yat prefs,
In our ye wode entryt, or yai wald cefs.
Thre wachmen fa, off wallis was cummyn new,
Within ye clofs ye Scotts fone yaim flew.
Or ony fcry was raiffit in yat ſtour,   1640
Douglace had tane ze zet off ye gret tour,
Rane up a grete, quhar at ye Captayne lay.
On fut he gat, and wald haiff beyn away;
Our lait it was; Douglace ſtrak up ye dur,
Bewfurd he fand into ye chawmyr flur,   1645
With a ſtyff fuerd to dede he has hym dycht;
Hys men folowit, yat worthy was and wycht.
Ye men yai flew, yat was into yair wanys,
Syne in ye clofs yai femblyt all at anys.
Ye houfs yai tuk, and Sothroune put to ded,   1650
Gat nane, bot ane, with lyff out off yat ſted,
For yat ze zett fa lang unſtekyt was.
Yis fpy he fled, till Durfder can pafs,
Tald yat Captayne, yat yai had hapnyt fa;
Another he gert into ye Enoch ga,   1655
In Tybris mur was warnyt off yis cafs,
And Lowchmaban all femblyt to yat place;
Ye cuntre raifs, quhen yai herd off fic thing,
To fege Douglace, and hecht yai fuld hym hyng.
Quhen Douglace wyſt na wayis fra yaim to chaip,
To failze hym he trowit yai wald yaim fchaip,
Dycfon he fend apon a curfour wycht
To warn Wallace, in all ye haiſt he mycht.
Off Lewyn-houfs Wallace had tayn in playn,

With

With thre hundreth gud men off mekill mayn; 1665
Kynfyth a Caftell, he thocht to wefy it,
Ane Rawynfdaill held, bot trew men leit hym wytt,
Yat he was owt yat tym off Cummyrnauld,
Lord Cumyn duelt on tribut in yat hauld.
Quhen Wallace wyft, he gert Erle Malcom ly 1670
With twa hundreth in a bufchment ner by,
To kepe ye houfs, yat nayn to it fuld fayr;
He tuk ye laiff, and in ye wode ner yar
A fcurrour he fet, to warn quhen he faw ocht.
Sone Rawynfdaill com, off yaim he had na thocht.
Quhen he was cumyn ye twa bufchments betweyn,
Ye fcurrour warnd ye cruell men and keyn;
Yan Wallace brak, and folowit on yaim faft.
Ye Sothroune fled, for yai war far agaft.
Rawynfdaill had yan bot fyffte men, 1680
Amang ye Scotts yair deids was litill to ken.
Quhen Erle Malcom had bard yaim fra ye place,
Na Sothroune zeid with lyff yat yai did grace.
Part Lennox men yai left ye horfs to ta,
On fpulzeyng yan yai wald na tary ma. 1685
To fege ye houfs yan Wallace couth not byd,
Throuchout ye land in awfull feyr yai ryd.
Yan Lithquow toun yai brynt into yair gayt,
Quhar Sothroune duelt, yai maid yair byggyngs hayt
Ye peyll yai tuk, and flew yat was yarin, 1690
Off Sothroune blud, ye Scotts thocht na fyn.
Syne on ye morn brynt Dawketh in a gleid,
Yan till a ftrenth in Newbottyll wode yai zeid.
Be yat Lawdir, and Cryftall off Cetoun,

Com fra ye bafs, and brynt Northallertoun   1695
For Inglifmen fuld yar na fuccour get;
Quha yai ourtuk, yai flew withoutyn lett.
To meit Wallace yai paft with all yair mycht,
A hundreth with yaim off men in armes brycht.
A blyth metyng yat tym was yaim betweyn,   1700
Quhen Erle Malcom and Wallace has yaim feyn.
Thom Dycfon yan was met with gud Wallace,
Quhilk grantyt fone to refkew Douglace.
Dycfon, he faid, wait yow yair multiple?
Thre thoufand men yair power mycht not be.   1705
Erle Malcom faid, though yai war thoufands fyffe,
For yis actioun methink yat we fuld ftryff.
Yan Hew ye Hay, yat duellyt undyr trewage
Off Inglifmen, fone he gaiff our ye wage,
Mar for to pay as yan he likyt nocht,   1710
With fyftye men with Wallace forth he focht;
To Peblis paft, bot na Sothroune yar baid,
Yan at ye Croice a playn fcry yai maid;
Wallace commaund, quha wald cum to hys pefs,
And byd yarat, reward fuld haiff but lefs.   1715
Gud Ryuirfurd, yat euir trew has beyn,
In Atryk wode, agayne ye Sothroune keyn,
Bydyn he had, and don yaim mekill der,
Saxte he led off nobill men in wer.
Wallace welcummyt quha com in hys fupple   1720
With Lordly feyr, and Chyftan-lik was he.
Yaim till aray yai zeid without ye toun,
Yair nowmyr was fex hundreth off renoun,
In byrneis brycht, all men off mekill waill,

            With

With glaid harts yai paſt in Clyddyſdaill. 1725
Ye ſege be yan was to ye Sawchar ſet,
Sic tithands com, quhilk maid yarin a let.
Quhen Sothroune hard yat Wallace was ſa ner,
Throw haiſty fray ye oft was all on ſter;
Na man was yar wald for ane oyir byd, 1730
Purpos yai tuk in Ingland for to ryd.
Ye chyftane ſaid, ſen yair King had befor,
Fra Wallace fled, ye cauſs was ye mor.
Faſt ſouth yai went, to byd it was gret waith.
Douglace as yan was quyt off yair ſcaith. 1735
In Crawfurd mur be yan was gud Wallace,
Quhen men hym tauld, yat Sothroune apon cace
Was fled away, and durſt nocht hym abyd.
Thre hundreth yan he cheſſyt with hym to ryd,
In lycht harnes, and horſs at yai wald waill. 1740
Ye Erle Makcom he bad byd with ye ſtaill,
To folow yaim, a bakgard for to be;
To ſtuff a chace in all haiſt bownyt he,
Throw Durſder he tuk ye gayneſt gayt,
Rycht fayn he wald off Sothroune mak debait. 1745
Ye playneſt way abowne Mortoun yai hald,
Kepand ye hycht, gyff yat ye Sothroune wald
Houſs to perfew, or cum to Lochmaban,
Bot tent yarto ye Ingliſmen tuk nan;
Done neth yai held, graith gydys can yaim leyr, 1750
Abowne Cloſbarn Wallace approchyt ner.
In ire he grew, quhen yai war in hys fycht,
To yaim he ſped with wyll and all yair mycht.
On a out part ye Scotts ſet in yat tyd,

Sewyn

Sewyn fcor at erd yai had fone at a fyd. 1755
Ye Sothroune faw yat it was hapnyt fa,
Turnyt in agayn refkew for to ma;
Quhen yai trowit beft agayn Scotland to ftand,
Erle Malcom com rycht ner at yair hand.
Ye haill power tuk playn purpofs to fle. 1760
Quha was at erd Wallace gert lat yaim be,
Apon ye formeft folowit in all hys mycht.
Ye Erle and hys apon ye laiff can lycht,
Dyd all to dede unhorfyt was yat tyd;
Feill men was flayn apon ye Sothroune fyd. 1765
Fyffe hundreth large or yai paft Dawfwintoun,
On Sothroune fyd to ded was brocht adoun.
Ye Scotts horfs mony began to tyr,
Suppos yaimfelff was cruell fers as fyr.
Ye flears left bathe wode and wattris haill, 1770
To tak ye playn yai thocht it maift awaill.
In gret battaill away full faft yai raid,
Into ftrenthis yai thocht to mak no baid.
Ner Louchmaban and Lothyrmofs yai went,
Befyd Throuchmaid, quhar feill Sothroune was fchent.
Rycht mony horfs, yat rounyng had falary,
And trawaillit fayr, yai mycht no furyir gang.
Schyr Jhon ye Grayme upon hys fut was fet,
Yan Wallace als lychtyt withoutyn let.
Yir twa on fute amang ye enemyfs zeid, 1780
Was nayn, but horfs, mycht fra yaim throw fpeid.
On Inglifmen fo cruelly yai focht,
Quhom yai ourtuk agayn harmyt us nocht.
To Wallace com a part off power new,

To

On reſtyt horſs, yat pertly couth perſew;   1785
Adam Corrie, with gud men off gret waill,
And Jhonſtone als, yat duelt in Hauſſdaill;
And Kyrkpatrik was in yat cumpany,
And Halyday, quhilk ſemblyt ſturdely:
Quhar yai entryt, ye ſailzie was ſo ſayr,   1790
Dede to ye ground feill frekis ſone yai ber.
Sewyn ſcor was haill off new cummyn men in deid,
Ye ſouth party off yaim had mekill dreid.
Wallace was horſſyt apon a curſour wycht,
At gud Corre had broucht into yair ſycht,   1795
To ſtuff ye chas with hys new chewalry;
He commaundyt Grayme, and all hys men for yi,
Togyddyr byd, and folow as yai mycht.
Thre Captaynis yar full ſone to dede he dycht.
Yat reſtyt horſs ſa wondyr weill hym bar,   1800
Quhom he ouirtuk agayne raiſs neuir mar;
Raithly he raid, and maid full mony wound,
Yir thre Captaynis he ſtikyt in yat ſtound,
Off Durſdeyr, Eneth, and Tybyr-mur.
Lord Clyffurds Eyme away to Clyffurd fur,   1805
Ye quhilk befor yat kepyt Lowchmaban;
Na landyt man chaipyt with hym bot ane;
For Maxwell als out off Carlauerok com,
Ont o ye Sothroune ye gayneſt way is gon;
In to ye chafs ſo wyſly yai rid,   1810
Few gat away yat come apon yat fide.
Beſyd Cokpull full feill fechtand yai fand,
Sum drownyt was, ſum ſlayn apon ye ſand;
Quha chapyt was in Ingland fled away.
                                         Wallace

Wallace raturnd, na prifoner tuk yai;   1815
In Carlauerok reftyng yat nycht yai maid,
Apon ye morn till Drumfres blythly raid;
Yar Wallace cryed, quha wald com till hys pefs,
Agayne Sothroune, yar malice for to cefs,
Till trew Scotts he ordand waryfoun,   1820
Quhar fawtyt had he granted remiffioun.
In Drumfres yan he wald na langar byd.
Ye Sothroune fled off Scotland on ilk fyd,
Be fey and land, without langar abaid,
Off caftellys, tounys, yan Wallace Chyftanys maid,
Rewlyt ye land, and put it into reft,
With trew keparys, ye quhilk he traiftyt beft.
Ye trew Douglace, yat I zow tald off ayr,
Kepar was maid fra Drumlanryk till Ayr:
Becaufs he had on Sothroune fic thing wrocht,   1830
Hyfs wyff was wraith, bot it fche fchawit nocht,
Undyr cowart hyr malice hyd perfyt,
As a fcherpent wats hyr tym to byt;
Till Douglace oft fche wrocht full mekill cayr,
Off yat as now I leyff quhill foryirmar.   1835
Bot Sothroune men durft her no caftell hald,
Bot left Scotland, befor as I yow tald,
Saiff ane Morton, a Captane fers and fell,
Yat held Dunde. Yan Wallace wald not duell,
Yiddyr he paft, and lappyt it about.   1840
Quhen Morton faw, yat he was in fic dout,
He afkyt leyff with yair lywys to ga.
Wallace denyit, and faid, it beis nocht fa,
Ye laft Captayne off Ingland yat her was,

I gaiff

I gaiff hym leyff with hys men for to pafs; 1845
Yow fall forthink fic maiftry for to mak,
All Ingland fall off ye exemple tak;
Sic men fra hym now to haiff worn,
Yow fall be hangyt, fuppofs yi King had fuorn.
He gert cummaund na Scotts fuld to yaim fpek, 1850
Conferme ye fege, and fo we fall us wrek
On Inglifmen, has fic will off Dunde
Scrymeour he maid yar conftable for to be.
A Ballingar off Ingland, yat was yar,
Paft out off Tay, and com to Whitbe far, 1855
To London fend, and tald off all yis cace,
Till hyng Morton wowyt had Wallace.
Befor yis tym Edwarde with power zeid
To wer in France, for yan he had no dreid;
Befor he trowyt Scotland fuld be hys awn. 1860
Quhen yai hym warnyt, quhow hys men was our thrawn,
Agayn he turnyt till Ingland haiftely,
And left hys deid all fekyt into fy.
Gafcone he clemyt as into heretage,
He left it yus, for all hys gret barnage; 1865
And Flanders als he thocht to tak on hand,
And yir he left, and come to reyff Scotland.
Quhen yat yis King in Ingland was cummyn hame,
Sowmounds yai maid, and chargyt Bruce be nayme,
And all oyir, yat leyffyt undir hys croun, 1870
Byfchop, Barroun, to cum at yair fummoun.
Quhen Wallace twyfs, throw Grace, had fred Scotland,
Yis tyran King tuk playnly apon hand,
For fic defyr, yat he mycht haiff no reft,

He

He thocht till hym off it to mak conqueft. 1875
In cowetyfs he had rongyng fo lang,
Chyftanes he maid; yat yai fuld nocht pafs wrang,
Gyds yai cheffyt, fra ftrenthis yaim to ghy,
Yai thocht no mor to byd at jeperty;
In playn battaill, and yai mycht Wallace wyn, 1880
He trowyt off wer yai wald na mor begyn.
Lat I yis King makand hys ordinans,
My purpofs is to fpek fumthing off Frans.
Ye Inglifmen, yat Gyan held at wer,
Till Franch folk yai did full mekill der. 1885
Kyng and confaill fone in yair witts keft,
To get Wallace yai thocht it was ye beft;
For Gyan land ye Inglifmen had yai;
Yai fchup yaim yus in all ye haift yai may:
For yai traiftyt, and Scotland war weill ftad, 1890
Wallace wald cum, as he yaim promyft had.
Ye famyn herrald, befor in Scotland was,
Yai hym cummaundyt, and ordand he fuld pafs
Into Scotland, without langar delay,
Out off ye Slus, as gudly as he may. 1895
Redy he was, in fchip he went on cace,
In Tayis mowth ye hawyn but baid he has;
Quhar Wallace was yan at ye failzie ftill,
And he refawyt ye harrold with gud will;
Yar wryt he raid, and faid hym on yis wyfs, 1900
Ane anfuer fone he couth yaim nocht dewyfs.
Till honeft inn ye harrolds yan he fend,
On Wallace coft rycht boundandly to fpend,
Quhill tym he faw how oyir mattris zeid,

An

An anfuer he fuld haive withoutyn dreid. 1905
Ye wytt off France thocht Wallace to commend,
Into Scotland, with yis harrold, yai fend,
Part off hys deid, and als ye difcriptioune
Off hym tane yar, be men off difcretioune,
Clerks, Knychts, and Harrolds, yat hym faw; 1910.
Bot I hereoff can nocht reherfs yaim aw.
Wallace ftatur, off gretnes, and off hycht,
Was jugyt yus, be difcretioun off fycht,
Yat faw hym, bath diffembill and in weid;
Nyne quarters large he was in lenth indeid; 1915
Thryd part lenth in fchuldrys braid was he,
Rycht fembly, ftrang, and lufty for to fe.
Hys lymmys gret, with ftalwart paifs and found,
Hys browis hard, hys armes gret and round;
Hys hand maid rycht lik till a pawmer, 1920
Off manlik, with nalefs gret and cler;
Proportionyt long and fayr was hys wefage,
Rycht fad off fpech, and abill in currage;
Braid breyft and heych, with fturdy crag and gret,
Hys lyppys round, hys noyfs was fquar and tret;
Bowand brow haryt, on brows and breis lycht,
Cler off eyn, lik dyamonds brycht;
Undyr ye chyn, on ye left fyd, was feyn,
Be hurt, a wain; hys colour was fangweyn;
Wounds he had in mony diuerfs place, 1930
Bot fayr and weill kepyt was hys face.
Off ryches he kepyt no propyr thing,
Gaiff as he wan lyk Alexander ye King.
In tym off pes, mek as a maid was he,

VOL. II.   P   Quhar

Quhar wer approchyt ye rycht Ector was he.   1935
To Scottſmen a gret credence he gaiff,
Bot knawin enemyſs yai couth hym nocht diſaiff.
Yir properteys war knawin into Frans,
Off hym to be off gud remembrans.
Mayſtir Jhon Blair yat patron couth reſaiff,   1940
In Wallace buk brewyt it with ye layff;
Bot he heroff as yan tuk litill heid,
Hys lauborous mynd was all on oyir deid.
At Dunde ſege yus ernyſtfully yai lay;
Tithands to hym Jop brocht on a day,
Quhow Edwarde, King with likly men to waill,
A hundyr thouſand, com for to aſſaill,
Yan Scotland ground yai had apon cace.
Into ſum part it grewyt gud Wallace.
He maid Scrymiour ſtill at ye houſs to ly,   1950
With twa thouſand, and chargit hym for yi,
Yat nayn ſuld chaip with lyff out off yat ſted,
At Sothroune war bot do yaim all to ded.
Scrymeour grantit rycht faithfully to byd;
With awcht thouſand Wallace couth fra hym ryd
To Santt Jhonſtoune, four dayis he graithyt hym yar,
With ſad awyſs towart ye ſouth can fayr.
For King Edwarde yat tym ordand had
Ten thouſand haill to paſs, yat was full glad,
With zong Wodſtok, a man off mekill mycht;   1690
At Stirlyng Bryg he ordand yaim full rycht,
And yar to byd, ye entre for to wer,
Off Wallace yan he trowit to haiff no der.
Yair leyff yai laucht, and paſt, but delay,

Rycht

Rycht far alyand, in a gud aray; 1965.
To Stirlyng com, and wald nocht lang abyd,
To fe ye north furth yan can he ryd,
Sic new curage fo fell in hys entent,
Quhilk maid Sothroune full far for to rapent.

   EXPLICIT LIBER NONUS
   ET INCIPIT DECIMUS.

※ The Manuscript has been so exactly copied, that some Contractions appear, which the writer of the M. S. had made use of for his own conveniency; such as,

at, for *that*, yhn, for *thine*. O, for *Oye*; ye, for *the*, *thee*. C, is frequently used for *S*; D, for *th*; ff, for *v*; o, for *Oo*, *u*; n, w, for *v*; z, for *y*, &c.

A.

A, *all, ah!*
Abowyn, *above*
Adill, *Atholl.* B. 7. v. 620
Agyt, *aged*
Allayne, *alone*
Als, *also, as*
Amange, *among*
Alay, *ally*
Ane our nowne, *one afternoon*
Angell hede, *angle head*
Annadyrdaill, *Annandale*
Aspre, *asper, sharp, rugged*
At, *that*
At he aw, *that which he owed*
Aw, *owed, belongs to*
Ayk, *oak*
Ayle, Faile, *the vulgar name of a religious house in Air*
Ayr, *heir*

B

BAID, *abode, stayed,* B. 9. v. 546, " Yar and I baid;" viz. *three have I stayed*
Bald, *bold*
Ballingar, *a kind of ship*
Balzoune, *Baliol*
Bandoune, *bond, obligation*
Bar, *bare, naked*
Barnage,

GLOSSARY.

Barnage, *Barons, baronage*
Bargane, *fight, contention*
Barrownys, *Barons*
Barrat, *hostile company*
Barrace, *bounds*
Basnet, *helmet, head-piece*
Basnat, *helmet*
Bayne, *bane, ready*
Bawk, *baulk, roof*
Bayle, *baleful*
Bears, *ancestors*
Be, *by*
Bellamy, *warlike man*
Beggar, *Biggar*
Bertane, *Britain*
Best, *beast*
Bery-abbey, *Bury-abbey*
Bestials, *engines for a siege*
Bikker, *hasty battle*
Biryness, *burial*
Bet, *supplied*
Birneys, *barns*
Blaw, *a blow*
Blent, *blinked, looked*
Bless, bleezes, *blaze, flame*
Boune, *ready prepared*
Bowis, *boughs*
Bowand, *bowing*
Borche, *to pledge, to pray*
Bodword, *message*

Boustous, *great, formidable*
Bownit, bownyt, *went, tended, made ready*
Boyd, B. 7. v. 25c, read
  Byrd
Bon, bane, *hurt, death*
Brukyt, *enjoyed*
Bradit, *forced*
Braithlye, *noisy, bravely, valiantly*
Brokill, *frail, doubtful*
Brachell, *bratchell*
Bertymit, *perished*
Bot, but, *without*
Bryg, *bridge*
Bryme, *brim, fierce*
Brygeane Cruk, *Bridge-end-Crook*
Bran, *brain*
Botts, *boats*
Browis, *brows*
Brewyt, *brieved*
Brim, *brother.* B. 9. v. 596
Brazars, *bracelets, armour for the arms*
Buskit, *prepared*
Bute, *advantage*
Burd, *board, table, plank*
Busk, *bush.* B. 3. v. 3
  froyte busk, *fruit bush*
      Burdeous,

GLOSSARY.

Burdeous, *Bourdeaux*
Burly, *large, rough, full*
But, *Isle of But*
Byrny, *corslet, hemlet*
Byrne, *burn*
Byrnand, *hot, burning*
Byrdyngs, *burdens*
Byrneis, *corselets*

C

Caiff, *Cave*
Chefs, *chose*
Child, *boy, page*
Churl, *strong man*
Chewyt, chevit, *atchieved*
Cefs, *to cease*
Cetown, *Seaton*
Chapyt, *escaped*
Caflies, cavillies, *lots*
Cornialis, *chronicles*
Condet, *conduct*
Corre, *currie*
Conschyrwyt, *conserved*
Couth, *could*
Cowart, *covert*
Conandly, *cunningly*
Courche, *kerchief, linen dress for the head*
Conquefs, *conquest*
Cordyt, *concorded*
Contre, *country*

Cornykle, *chronicle*
Crummade, *Cromarty*
Cragevyum, *Cragunyn.* B. 7. v. 649
Cuk, cok, *centinel*
Crawis, *crabs*
Cunnel-bane, *collar-bone*
Cur, *cure*
Cultir-hoppis, *Cultir-hope*
Cummerit, *encumbered*

D

Dait, *time*
Dauch, daw, *lazy, idle*
Dede, *death*
Der, *injury*
Dewory, *devoir, duty*
Dipplyne, *Duplin near Perth*
Dern, *dark, concealed*
Defs, *desk, seat, table*
Deit, *died*
Derfly, *strongly*
Douir, *Dover*
Down, *Down Castle*
Drychyn, dreiching, *drawing, tarrying*
Dreich, *slowly, at a distance*
Durplin, *Duplin near Perth*
Dykis,

GLOSSARY.

Dykis, *trenches*
Dyrk, *dark*

E

Effer, *appearance*
Ellys, *else*
Erewyn, *Irvine*
Erfche, *Irish*
Etlyt, *aimed*
Eyme, *uncle*

F

Fadrs, *fathers*
Fais, *foes*
Familiar, *of the same nation or kindred*
Fand, *found*
Far, *fair*
Fafteing, *a fting or pole faftened*
Faffoun, *fashion*
Fayis, *foes*
Faw, *fall*
Faggaldys, *faggots*
Ferfe. B. 9. v. 1564, *furname of Lady Douglas*
"Feill at ze leid fall erar lofs ye lyff." B. 7. v. 868, viz. *Many that you lead, shall earlier lofe the life*
Ferd, *fourth*

Ferdely, *feardly*
Fey, *fatal, unfortunate, unhappy*
Fewtir, *in ranks*
Feid, *feud, hatred, quarrel*
Feill fyfs, *many times*
Fewtir, *felt, became*
Feryt, *became*
Feld, *field*
Feill, *many*
Fevirzer, *February*
Fellaft, *fierceft*
Fellis, *fails*
Flytting, *removing*
Floryng, *florins*
Flothis, *floods*
Forrown, *forerun*
Foryours, *forragers*
Forfychan, *Torphichen*
Forrag, *forage, reconnoitre*
Forn, *food*
Foreft Kirk, *Selkirk*
Foftyr, *fofter, nourish*
Forfye, *for force*
Fra, *from*
Truftir us, *fruftrate*
Frekis, *fports, whims*
Frekis, *light follows*
Frawart, *from, froward, fromward*

Fryfaill,

GLOSSARY.

Fryſaill, Frazer, *a ſurname*
Freich, *to free*
Fygourt, *figured*
Fyfe, *five*
Fur, *fare, make uſe of.*

G

GA, *go*
Gadalos, *Gadalis*
"Gaddrys off ye gawdy fer," B. 1c. v. 342, in a former printed edition, *Gadders of Gaudifer*
Ganze, *javelin, arrow*
Gargownno, *Gargunnock*
Garraid, *Gerard*
Garth, *yard, incloſure*
Garmand, *ganand, fit, proper*
Gardoune, *juriſdiction*
Gart, *cauſed*
Ger, *accoutrements*
Gert on, *cauſed one*
Geyeler, *Jaylor*
Gowlis, *gules, red*
Glowis, *gloves*
Glamrous, *clamorous*
Greis, *grey colour*
Grete, *grate.* B. 7. v. 67
Gre, *degree*
Grathis, *clothes*

Gyrth, *gerth, refuge*
Gyllſland, *Guilderland*
Guana, Gyan, *Guienne.*

H

HABOUNDANLE, *abundantly*
Haddyr, *heath*
Haile, *whole*
Haboundyt, *abounded*
Halfe, *throat, neck*
Harn-pan, *ſkull*
Hard, *heard*
Harns, *brains*
Hathyngtown, *Haddington*
Haldyn, *holden, eſteemed*
Hals, *throat, neck*
He, *high*
Heith, *high*
Heaſt, *higheſt*
Her, *heir.* B. 7. v. 41
Herbyage, *harbourage, retreat*
Her, *here*
Hewynnis, *heavens*
Hecht, *denominated*
Hangyt, *hanged*
Hint, *took*
Ho, *ſtop*
Howlat, *owl*
Hoo, *interruption*

GLOSSARY.

Hyr, *heir*
Hydwyfs, *hideous, terrible*
Hynt, *pulled, lifted.*

I

IN, ufed for *and*, B. i. v. 112
Imbaffet, *ambaffador*
Inwey, *envy*
Innys, *inn*
Inlumyt, *illuminate*
Joppis-bog, B. 6. v. 705. *Roppis-bog*
Jowell, *jewel.*

K

KAMYSKYNETT, *abbey of Cambus Kenneth*
Kerwyt, *carved*
Keft, *caft*
Kingace, *Kincace*
Kneland, *furname of Cleland*
Kyll, *Kyle*
Kynrick, *kingdom*
Kyth, *Kythe, fhewed, appeared.*

L

LATT, *let, ftop, hinder*
Lattyn, *hindrance*
Lawit, *low.* B. 5. v. 156

Law, *low*
Lawte, *humblenefs*
Ledys, *Leeds*
Lemand, leme, *gleam, flame*
Lekle, *Leckie near Gargunnock, Stirling-fhire*
Ledaill, *Liddifdale*
Leryt, *learned*
Leit, *let*
Lewyng, living, *fuftenance*
Levir, levar, *rather*
Lewyfs, *leaves of trees*
Leythand, *fighing*
Lewit, levit, *allowed, granted*
Lewyn-houfe, *Lennox.* B. 11. v. 823.
Lieffe, *live, leave*
Licaym, *limbs.*
Longcaftle, *Lancafter*
Locklute, *lock. d*
Longcafchyr, *Lancafhire*
Lorn, *loft*
Lund, *London*
Lugit, *lodged*
Lundors, *Lundores-abbey*
Luff-burd, *loof-board*
Lyflat, *the very fame*
Lynt, *lint, flax.*

MA,

GLOSSARY.

M

MA, *more*
Macht, *matcht*
Mar, *mayor*
Maſt, *moſt*
Mayne, *moan*
May, *more*
Matelent, *rage, great deſire*
Mayre, *Mary*
Mayre ſcheyne. B. 2. v. 336, *for the ſake of the glorious, or virgin Mary*
Maters, materis, *matrons, mothers*
Meſſan wode, *Methven wood*
Mernys, *Merns near Glaſgow*
Melle, *conteſt, battle*
Menys, *moans, complains*
Mete, *meet*
Mekill, *much*
Modyr, *mother*
Mony, *many*
Miſdears, *miſ-doers, evildoers*
Mur, *demure*
Myſtred, *needed*

N

NERCH, *March*. B. 10 v. 101, Counteſs of March.
Neuo, *nephew*
Nounys, *nuns*
Noune, *noon*
Noyir, *neither*.

O

O, Oye, *grandchild*
Ochtell, *Ochill-hills*
Ogart, *terror*
Or, *before, ere*
Oft-ſyiſs, *oft-times*
Oſt, *hoſt*
Our-lord, *over-lord*
Outrage, *outrageous*
Our-heyde, *overtook*
Our, *over*
Oyir, *other*
Oychall, *Ochill-hills*
Oyſs, *uſe, cuſtom, practice.*

P

PALZEON, *tent*
Pape, *Pope*
Par, *impair*
Peſs, *peace*
Peill, *fort, caſtle*
Pepe, *Pope*

Purway,

GLOSSARY.

Purway, *purvey*
Pissand, *puissant, strength*
Pout-staff, *strong staff*
Poille, *Pole*
Prophesye out, B. 2. v. 169 in the printed editions. *A per se of*
Powed, *pulled*
Prynsnall, *principal*
Pute, *pity*
Pur no rik, *poor nor rich*
*** *No Englishman would deem them acting amiss, poor nor rich. B. 5. v. 378*
Pyt, *to pity.*

R

RA, Rae, *a surname* B. 1c. v. 454
Racunnyss, *recognize*
Rang, range, *rank, order*
Rabutyt, rebutit, *repulsed*
Rapys, *ropes*
Ragment, *discourse, collection, treaty*
Ray, *song of triumph, array*
Raw, *row, rank*
Rawllit, *ruled*
Ramuff, *remove*
Rede, reid, *counsel, read*
Reik, *smoke*
Reury, reevery, *robbery*
Rerd, *clamour, noise*
Rad, *afraid*
Rew, *repent, regret*
Roman, *Roman use.* B. 1c. v. 1003, *Roman Church Service*
Rodds, *Rhodes Island*
Royd, *void.* B. 5. v. 77
Rouschede, *rushed*
Rought, *attained*
Rok, *distaff*
Roy, *king*
Rouch-rowlyngs, *rulzions, brogues, or, open shoes untanned*
Rik, *rich*
Repende, *rampart*
Ruthly, *sorely*
Ruff, *roof*
At Ruff, *under roof*
Ruwan, *Ruthven*
Rudyrfurd, *Rutherfurd*
Ryk, *kingly, kingdom*
Ryvirfurd, *Rutherford.*

S

SA, *so*
Saffir, *sapphire*

Salk,

GLOSSARY.

Salk, *sake*
Salt, *a fault*
Sawely, *alone, solely*
Said, *to trouble, to make sore*
Sawit, *saved*
Saw, *a saying, to declare;* B. 2. v. 304, " for a-wenture might saw," *as adventure might shew*
Salt, *assault*
Sanct Johnstoune, *Perth*
Sanyt, *healed, saved*
Sanct Beis Hede, *St Bay's Head*
Sawcher, *Sanquhar*
Sey, *trial, proof, tasting*
Sessoun, *season*
Senzeit, *feigned.* B. 5. v. 926
Semle, *assembly*
Sey, *sea*
Swyr, sware, *the neck*
Sekar, *cut*
Scir, sere, *sore several, many*
Se, *see*
Serd, *served*
Sily, *silly*
Sent, *send*
Sentryss, gentrice, *gentility, generosity*
Sellis, *cells*
Scroggy, *thorny, bushy*
Schyff, schryve, *confess*
Senzie, Signior, *Lordship* B. 10. v. 139
Schot, *put forth, launched*
Schoys, *shoes*
Schaw, *a surname,* B. 6. v. 70
Schent, *sent, confounded*
Scry sone rais, " *the cry soon raise,*" B. 4. v. 671
Sembled, *assembled*
Scor, *twenty*
Scule, *School*
Scaithis, *hurts, injuries*
Sedane, *sudden*
Serwis, *deserves*
Sekar, *cut*
Schonkit, *shaked*
Scansyt, *scanned*
Scrymmags, scrymage, *skirmish in sport*
Scheyne, schene, *clean, shining, beautiful*
Seildyn, *seldom*
Semly, *handsome.*
Shaw, *a wood or grove*
Sitful, *sorrowful*

Sekar,

GLOSSARY.

Sekar, *sure, certain*
Siyfs, *assize*
Sophammis, *sophisms*
Syng, *sign*
Sone, *soon*
Soudly, *suddled*
Sperd, *asked, enquired*
Souzhe, or souch, *noice*
Slonk, *Slough, ditch, marshy ground*
Sleid, staid, *den, valley*
Segs, *seges, men*
Sper, *spear*
Snell, *sharp, keen*
Spayn, *spoon*
South-gait, *South-street*
Slewit, *slipped*, B. 7. v. 207
Slew fyre, *struck fire*
Sowmir, *sumpter horse*
Souerty, *surety*
Stark, sterk, *strong*
Stragyll, *straggle*
Se, *so*
Stynt, stint, *stop, delay*
Strowbill, *trouble, troublesome*
Stewyn, steven, *mouth, voice, sound*
Stewyn, *Steven*
Stall, *stole*

Staill, stale, *separate party, ambush, secret place*
Stapill, *stable, sure*
Stark, *stout*
Stikyt, *sticked, stabbed*
Sle, *sly*
Streftly, *fully*
Stark, stur, *stout and brave*
Steide, stede, *place, condition*
Stuart, *steward*
Stelled, stolled, *flowed*
Swyth, *swift*
Suerd, *sword*
Swa, *so*
Suete, *sweat*
Swappyt, *snapped, drew*
Swak, swake, *a throw, shock*
Swyth, *quickly*
Syfe, feis, *possession*
Swaket, *cast*
Syn, *after*
Syn, *there, next*

T.

TA, *take*
Tawkand, *talking*
Tirandry, *tyranny*
Teyn, *sorrow, hurt, anger*
Terand, *tyrant*

Thryllage,

GLOSSARY.

Thre, *three*
Thryllage, *vaſſalage*
Thewittil, *whittle, ſhort knife*
The, *thigh*
Thruſande, *burniſhed*
Tholyt, *ſuffered, endured*
Thigged, *begged*
Till, *to, unto*
To, *too*
To *is frequently uſed for in*, as, Left ye lyff to wed, *left their life in wed.* B. 4. v. 6 3.
Tournberry, *Turnbury*
Topaſtone, *Topaz ſtone*
Towboth, *Priſon*
Traſtyt, *truſted*
Trewis it words tak, B. 3. v. 271. *It behoves us to take truce*
Tranontit, traventit, *marched ſuddenly*
Tre, *tree, timber*
Tvthings, *tidings*
Turfs *be carried haſtily*
Tynt, *loſt*

V

UMQUHILL, *ere while, formerly*

Unruboytyt, unrebytyt, *unrepulſed*
Unſowerable, *inſufferable*
Uſs, *uſe*
Utaſs, *octaves.* B. 6. v. 1
Vikyt, *irked, feared.*

W

WA, *ſorrow, ſorry*
Waith, *waif, goods found or unowned*
Wala, *valley*
Waite, *wote*
Waille, *vale*
Wailland, *chooſing*
Waillis, *Wales*
War, *aware*
Warlage, *deed of valour*
Waill, *value*
Wappynys, *weapons*
Wauntyt, *amiſſing*
Waynys, *veins*
Wayne, *home, habitation*
Warnage or vernage, *domeſtic food*
Waryit, *accurſed*
War, *were*
Wanyſs, wanes, *places of abode*
Wawerand wynd, *wavering wind*
Wageourſs,

GLOSSARY.

Wageourſs, *mercenaries*
Wer, *war, warlike expedition, wear*
Werray, *very*
Weſtermar, *farther weſt*
Wend, *to go*
Weild, *guide or manage*
Wenys, *thinkeſt*
Wedeis, *withes, twigs*
Wed, *pledge*
Weryte, *verity*
Wend, weened, *imagined*
Weildand weylle, *well as he could wiſh*
Wer, ver, *spring*
Weyne, ween, but weyne, *without doubt*
Weſche, *waſh*
Wicht, *valiant, ſtrong*
Wicke, *wrack, revenge*
Wittaill, *victual*
Wincuſt, *vanquiſhed*
"William Lang Douglace," *William Dougles Lang, &c.* B. 10. v. 1109
Wok, *walked*
Wower, *vower, woer*
Woo, *wo, ſorrowful*

Wowyn, *woven*
Wownnand, *winning, dwelling*
Worthit to weide, *became frantic*
Worthis, *waxes*
Worth, *grew, became*
Worthit, *waxed*
Wrokyn, *wreaked, avenged*
Wrandly, *like to ſwarm or flock*
Wycht with, *ſtrong*
Wyrking, *working.*

Y

YAN, *then, than,*
Ymage, *homage*
Yne action, B. 3. v. 363 in former editions "*thine nation*"
Yocht, *thought*
Yrage, *Iriſh*
Yrk, irk, *fear, weariness*

Z

ZA, *yea yes*
Zeid, *went*
Zett, *yet, gate, door*
Zhetts, *yets, gates*
Zuheyll, *wheel.*

www.ingramcontent.com/pod-product-compliance
Lightning Source LLC
Chambersburg PA
CBHW031439160426
43195CB00010BB/783